# Praise for *Climbing the Ladder in Stilettos*

"Though I know nothing about stilettos, I do know good business practices, and so does Lynette Lewis. In *Climbing the Ladder in Stilettos* she offers insightful strategies that will positively impact your work. Every woman needs to read this book!"

JOHN C. MAXWELL
*New York Times* Best-Selling Author and Speaker
Founder of INJOY Stewardship Services and Equip

"Books and shoes are my weakness! After reading this practical guide to success in your career and personal life, you might agree as you 'pair' the combo. How beneficial to use them as a competitive strength!"

GABRIELA FERRARI
Global Business Intelligence, Nike

"A fun read and worth it!"

GENEVIEVE BOS
Co-Founder and Publisher, *PINK* Magazine

"Lynette is a national treasure! Not only did she inspire and motivate our CEO's, but she also equipped them with practical, proven tools that they could use to connect their corporate purpose to the individual purpose of each of their team members."

LANE A. KRAMER
President, The CEO Institute

"As a frequent speaker for the Leadership Forum, Lynette Lewis is always a powerhouse of seasoned expertise, savvy insight, and fun. Now she puts these same ideas to paper, a gift to every reader! Speaking or writing, she captivates an audience like few others I know."

CAROLE HYATT
Founder and CEO, The Leadership Forum

*"Climbing the Ladder in Stilettos* is a fabulous strategic framework for achieving professional and personal fulfillment that draws on real life experiences."

CELINA REALUYO
Former Senior U.S. Diplomat and
Goldman Sachs International Banker

"Lynette Lewis has compiled magnificent lessons, valuable insights, and sound strategies for women eager to advance their careers, and more importantly, to find joy and satisfaction at work."

JOYCE ROCHÉ
President and CEO, Girls Incorporated

# CLIMBING
## the
# LADDER
## in
# Stilettos

# CLIMBING
the
# LADDER
in
# Stilettos

Ten Strategies for Stepping Up
to Success and Satisfaction at Work

LYNETTE LEWIS

THOMAS NELSON
*Since 1798*

NASHVILLE   DALLAS   MEXICO CITY   RIO DE JANEIRO   BEIJING

CLIMBING THE LADDER IN STILETTOS

© 2006 Lynette Lewis

Published in Nashville, Tennessee, by Thomas Nelson. Thomas Nelson is a registered trademark of Thomas Nelson, Inc.

Thomas Nelson, Inc. titles may be purchased in bulk for educational, business, fund-raising, or sales promotional use. For information, please e-mail SpecialMarkets@ThomasNelson.com.

Cover Design: Karen Williams
Page Design: Mandi Cofer
Acquisitions Editor: Debbie Wickwire
Managing Editor: Adria Haley

### Library of Congress Cataloging-in-Publication Data

Lewis, Lynette.
    Climbing the ladder in stilettos : ten strategies for stepping up to success and satisfaction at work / Lynette Lewis.
        p. cm.
    Includes bibliographical references.
    ISBN 978-0-8499-0186-7 (hardcover)
    ISBN 978-1-5955-5144-3 (trade paper)
    1. Women—Vocational guidance. 2. Women in the professions.
3. Women—Promotions. I. Title.
HF5382.6.L49 2006
    650.1082—dc22

                                                                            2006025932

*Printed in the United States of America*
09 10 11 12 13 QW 8 7 6 5 4 3 2

*I joyfully dedicate this book to my parents—*


*Geneva Troyer*
*Mom, you're my lifelong best friend.*
*For forty-four years, your love, comfort, and prayers have*
*carried the constant, joyful theme of "Yes!"*


*Howard Troyer*
*Dad, you are wisdom, character, and faith personified.*
*You taught me about the world of business.*
*Without saying a word, your life shouts success.*

# CONTENTS

# Contents

# Acknowledgments

I wanted to write a book but didn't know how. These are the gifted artists who helped turn an average voice into a symphony.

*Esther Fedorkevich.* From our first conversation over coffee at 50th and Broadway, your enthusiasm and confidence have kept me believing. I am so grateful for you.

*Amy Gregory.* You took my many random ideas and molded them into one concept that made sense. What a talent you are!

*Brent Cole.* My coach and guide. Thanks for the excellent education and for the calm confidence you brought on all those Friday mornings.

*Angel Wolfe.* Tireless even after midnight, you parachuted in at just the right moment and added so much.

# Acknowledgments

*Debbie Wickwire.* Meeting you has been my favorite gift in all of this! You are the epitome of professionalism and a treasured new friend. Thank you for helping craft and carry the vision for this book from day one.

*The Thomas Nelson team.* I've heard of publishing nightmares, but you have been a dream. Thank you for taking the seeds of an idea and making them great.

*Eutha Godfrey, Genie Lewis, Lois Cox, Pam Pulsfort, Alice Rhee, and Katye Rone.* Someday a full accounting of your investments will be adequately rewarded. Thank you for the strength of your agreement, for every note and every call.

*Carole Hyatt.* You generously brought so many incredible women to this project. I am filled with gratitude for you—mentor, encourager, partner, and friend.

*The MSNY and KPIC families.* If you see me dabbing my eyes on Sundays, it's because I'm overwhelmed at the privilege of doing life with you.

*Nathan, Christian, Jordan, and JohnLuke.* You are the most treasured surprise gifts of all time. Thanks for being genuinely interested in this story.

*My husband and soul mate, Ron.* You are my over-and-above-all-I-asked-or-hoped-for love! Thank you for your joyful smile that continually says, "Go for it!"

*And God, my Savior.* This is all for Your glory. I am humbled You would open doors as rich and satisfying as these.

# Women and Our Shoes

**R**iding the subways of New York City each week, I'm amazed at how many women wear one pair of shoes *to* work, change into another pair *at* work, and carry yet another pair for plans *after* work.

Our lives as working women can often be reflected in our collection of shoes. We have so many roles and so many shoes to fill.

I often think of a friend who was asked to fill a bag with items that would help the others in her group at a leadership event understand more about who she is. She filled the bag with a dozen shoes and described the experiences she'd had wearing each one: the running shoes she wore in a marathon, the sensible heels in which she defended her PhD dissertation, and her favorite pair of stilettos worn at a black-tie event where she received an achievement award.

Ah yes, we do enjoy our shoes. Last year, American women spent nearly $17 *billion* on fashion footwear between October 2004 and October 2005. If you think that sounds like a lot, you're right; it's a 10 percent increase over the year before![1]

Now, when you want to climb a ladder, you don't typically slip on a pair of stilettos. Some would say you can't or shouldn't, insisting, "Climbing ladders is dangerous. It's a man's job, and it requires rubber-soled shoes."

> Regardless of how we describe it, climbing the corporate ladder is simply this: a real challenge.

Likewise, advancing a career as a woman is no simple task. It can be a slippery slope. There is juggling involved and a great deal of balance required. But regardless of how we describe it, climbing the corporate ladder is simply this: a real challenge.

The title of this book is a metaphor for the challenges women face in today's working world. Climbing a ladder (a typically masculine task) in stilettos (a feminine fashion icon) sounds almost laughable. At the very least, it sounds more like a circus feat than a legitimate endeavor. For years, that's how it felt for me. Some days, it still does.

Nevertheless, if we believe in our path, we should continue moving upward with our collection of shoes in tow.

Personally, I'm not a big fan of ladders. Just the other afternoon while helping my husband hang new curtains in our living room, I had to climb a ladder and found it quite precarious, even in running shoes.

I am, however, a fan of stilettos. Though I certainly don't wear them every day, and rarely at work, my stilettos tend to accompany the many roles I play:

- the professional in conservative black stilettos with a gray pencil skirt and silk button-down blouse;
- the single woman, and later the wife, wearing strappy stilettos with a favorite dinner dress;
- the fun-loving friend on a Friday night in leopard-print stilettos with designer jeans.

## Women and Our Shoes

Amid the many roles you also play, thank you for picking up this book. I am honored that you would take some of your very precious time to walk with me through these pages. Ideally, rather than you reading, I wish we were together in person, chatting over a cup of coffee or a glass of iced tea out on my front porch.

I'd ask you how you've been doing lately. Are you fulfilled in your work? What has been on your heart as you think about how and where you spend your days? Do you have a sense of expectancy and joy about the future? What are your greatest challenges? Tell me about your children or your latest travels. If you could do anything in the world without the fear of failing, what would you do?

I think we'd find that we have much in common. As women, we hope for many of the same things, worry over similar trials, and long for more time and meaning and joy. We'd probably laugh as we share common experiences and get teary-eyed as we talk about the times we wondered how we'd ever make it through.

Perhaps someday our paths will cross, and you and I will have the pleasure of meeting in person. In the meantime, we can carry on our conversation in the pages of this book. I will ask you much about yourself and in return will offer you insights into my personal journey of climbing the proverbial ladder. I've done it as a single woman, a wife, a new mother, and a professional who highly values her work.

It has by no means been a storybook climb. There have been seasons filled with unanswered questions and anger at closed doors and delays. There have also been times of deep joy and opportune surprise. There have been days when I didn't feel like I was going anywhere.

I personally never intended to step up the corporate ladder. I figured I'd work a few years out of college at something fun and then meet the man of my dreams, get married, and have the luxury of choosing whether or not to continue working.

My story turned out to be much different than I expected. Yet after twenty-two years in the corporate world, I recognize patterns of thinking and working that have enabled me to find an abiding joy and satisfaction along the way. These are lessons sometimes learned the hard way, lessons I now share when speaking to women of all ages and vocations throughout each year. I have by no means done it perfectly, but I have adjusted along the way and stayed the course.

On the pages that follow, you will hear many stories in addition to my own. I will introduce you to some incredible women. They include new and old friends, some of whom are longtime mentors who from near and far have taught me many of the strategies I will share on the pages to come: Bridgette Heller, president of the global baby and kids division of Johnson & Johnson; Cecily Truett, sixteen-time Emmy-winning television producer; Sylvia Hatchell, head women's basketball coach for the University of North Carolina; and Denise Johnston, president of the adult division at The Gap. These are just a few of the women whose stories I hope will also inspire you in specific, practical new ways.

> You are designed for greatness. Your heart, mind, spirit, and soul do not easily accommodate mediocrity.

I invite you to take in each story and every lesson, reflecting on how you can apply them to your own career and life. These are women like you and me who hope for all the joy, meaning, success, and satisfaction that are available to us if we know where to look for them and how to look at them. Why would we spend the majority of our waking hours doing something that yields anything less?

There are a couple of key premises throughout the book that I should mention before we get started. The first is that *you are designed for greatness.* Your heart, mind, spirit, and soul do not easily accommodate mediocrity. Something inside of each of us yearns to be set apart from the crowd, to be recognized for something significant, to be able to achieve in ways that set a new standard of excellence and inspire those watching to do the same for themselves.

I'm a personal fan of the cable channel HGTV (Home and Garden Television). I love watching professional designers work with ordinary people to transform their lackluster homes into things of beauty. It's fascinating to see what a few creative ideas and minimal investments can do to bring a room or home to a place of beauty and greatness.

Our lives are often so similar. There is a place of excellence and greatness that awaits us if we can just rally the right resources to help us get there. My hope is that this book in your hands will be one of those resources, helping you craft a new vision of what your life at work can be, providing ideas and practical tools for beginning today on a journey to the most satisfying and rewarding life possible, on and off the job.

The second premise is that *we are all waiting and yearning for something.* You may be at a place of contentment in every area of your life. If so, be grateful because you are not in the majority. Most of us are still longing for something significant in one or more areas of our lives. It may be for a crucial promotion, for our wayward children to return home, for the relationship of our dreams to emerge, to have a baby, to get through our physical setbacks . . . The list goes on and on.

It is the tension between our vision of greatness and the challenges of waiting that often brings discouragement and stress. We miss the simple joys of today and often experience years of discontentment. This tension is evident in statistics such as these:

- 60 percent of women participate in the U.S. labor force.
- 40 percent of working women work evenings, nights, or weekends on a regular basis, and 33 percent work shifts different than their spouses or partners.
- 23 percent of women executives and professionals, globally, say they feel "super-stressed."
- 25 percent of mothers who work full-time and have children under thirteen feel stress almost every day.[2]

The tension in my own life compelled me to search with resolve to find a place of satisfaction and joy. I laughed, cried, prayed, and spent hours talking with hundreds of women en route to discovering a few key tools that, after much testing, have proven to reap tangible rewards and sustainable results.

Here on these pages are some of those women and a few of the tools we have acquired along the way. It's certainly not an exhaustive list, but perhaps it is enough to give you some key insights that will inspire a sense of expectancy and motivation in your own career journey, regardless of where you are now.

Thank you for the pleasure of your company. I hope that the time you invest here yields a great reward in your daily life. We are on this journey together, still learning and still climbing, always considering just which shoes we ought to wear!

*I stopped one day after reviewing a video I had just produced for IBM. It was a huge project; I had traveled to three continents, around the world in three weeks. It was a whirlwind, so thrilling and exciting. I'm sitting on my sofa, viewing the results, and realizing that I cannot relate to this piece of videotape. I cannot hug it or relate to it.*

—ANNE PAGE
President, APFilms

# ONE

# Why Am I Working?

I still remember that Monday morning in August. It was a blistering hot day in Manhattan, even in the early morning hours. I spent the typical hour getting ready, doing my hair, and making sure my makeup was just right. I had my coffee and smoothie and then headed out the door.

Just as I entered the subway station, the train was pulling away. I groaned, knowing exactly what that meant. The next eight minutes were like standing in a sauna. I'm sure the guy next to me thought he heard a faucet running, but no, it was just the sweat draining inside my blouse while my hair was frizzing up by the minute.

I rode the subway to 50th Street and then waited for the bus for ten minutes while the heat and humidity did further damage. The bus arrived and drove the two miles to the ferry station. But just as the bus pulled into the station, the ferry pulled out. Another twenty-minute wait. What would it be next?

I knew I'd be late to work, and at this point I couldn't fathom the thought of going to the office at all.

By the time I finally arrived, I was a mess inside and out. My hair and outfit were ruined. I was exhausted from the commute. As I sat down at my desk in Jersey City overlooking the skyline of downtown Manhattan, negative thoughts flooded my head.

*No one really appreciates me around here. Why am I working here anyway? They don't know my dreams, what I really want to be and do. I work hard, put in the hours, give them my best energy of the day, and for what? A paycheck that doesn't feel like enough? Stress over having to please so many people?*

The discouragement brought me to tears. I knew I had to pull myself together. I wasn't being paid to waste time crying at my desk. But how could I lift myself out of this sense of despair?

At that point I serendipitously thought of the young woman sitting in the office next door. Sandra and I had met the first day I started in the Jersey City office. I was her manager, and over the course of the last year, we'd become more than just colleagues; we were friends. I helped her discover some of her dreams and worked with her to map out a plan to align her job with those dreams. She had developed significantly that year, and the satisfaction I felt from having helped her was deeply rewarding.

Thinking of Sandra through my tears helped lift the heaviness. Perhaps she was one of the main reasons I was doing this job and working hard day after day.

Sandra often told me, "You are a gift, Lynette. You've helped me find my way." Recalling this reminded me that my efforts were worth it. Helping people and changing lives do matter. This realization helped me get back in touch once again with the real reason I was working.

## THE CHALLENGE: I NEED TO
## FIND MEANING IN THE JOB I HAVE NOW

Have you ever felt like I did on that Monday morning? There are times when a good job and an adequate paycheck aren't enough for the energy and inconvenience it takes to get through the workday.

Often in times like this we feel especially alone. Everyone else around us appears to be coping quite well. We may look like we're coping, but inside we wonder how long we can keep going. Can we find something that's better aligned with our bigger ideas and dreams? It's probably one of the most common, and important, questions people ask.

An extremely popular book in recent history is Rick Warren's *The Purpose-Driven Life*. In fact, at the time of this writing, it is the all-time best-selling nonfiction hardback in America. This speaks volumes about where Americans find themselves in their work spectrum—most feel there is still something more to life than just work.

The success of Warren's book falls in line with a study conducted by the Barna Research Group, which shows that half of Americans are "searching for meaning and purpose in life."[1] Author Os Guinness concurs. In his book *The Call: Finding and Fulfilling the Central Purpose of Your Life*, Guinness explains, "Deep in our hearts, we all want to find and fulfill a purpose bigger than ourselves. Only such a larger purpose can inspire us to heights we know we could never reach on our own. For each of us the real purpose is personal and passionate: to know what we are here to do, and why."[2]

Answering the "why" question is essential if we want to have rich, deep meaning in our careers. Women in particular seem to have something inside our hearts that demands we answer this question. We are made for meaning; we thrive by making a difference and helping others, by seeing our kids grow up to be successful adults who will make an impact on the world.

> Answering the "why" question is essential if we want to have rich, deep meaning in our careers.

The reality, however, is that it's not easy to derive this deeper meaning from our work. Some individuals, certainly in the minority, know what their purpose is early in life. They see themselves doing something great and find it natural to forge a pathway to get there. They arrive in their twenties or earlier, when the rest of us are just beginning to realize we've been asking the wrong questions— or not questioning anything at all.

Most of us simply find ourselves on a certain path or in what someone else might call a "career." Yet outside of financial provision, this career often seems void of deep significance. We might have a college education or vocational training or now, after years of working, various experiences and company titles that are scattered across our résumés.

But all these credentials don't necessarily bring meaning; they don't easily come together in answering that all-important question that hangs somewhere in the background: Why?

Why this job? Why these coworkers? Why these responsibilities in this place at this time? Why not something else? Something better? The questions beg for answers—not regularly perhaps, but occasionally, like on a bad day when it's hot outside and you miss the train.

## UNCOVERING YOUR PURPOSE

My dear friend Anne Page, president of her own communications company, and I were chatting awhile ago. She described a personal epiphany she had a few years ago, one that occurs for many women after years of working on their careers.

> I stopped one day after reviewing a video I had just produced for IBM. It was a huge project; I had traveled to three continents, around the world in three weeks. It was a whirlwind, so thrilling and exciting. I'm sitting on my sofa, viewing the results, and realizing that I cannot relate to this piece of videotape. I cannot hug it or relate to it. It was such a successful project, such a pinnacle, and it was done. I could show a video, but it was just a video; it wasn't helping me live my life as a whole person. What a lonely and sad moment. At forty-seven, I realized there was a lot I had missed. Somehow I had it wired that this was what I had to do to be successful. So I had to ask, "Is this success, sitting in my living room with this video?" It may be a successful career, but not a successful life.[3]

This epiphany moment led Anne to make significant changes in her life, ultimately finding more time for relationships (she met and married her soul mate) and taking time for other personal pursuits (fixing up their home). These changes have enhanced her career success while bringing greater satisfaction than ever before. In short, Anne discovered a deeper sense of purpose.

Purpose is a topic I've been studying in depth over the last five years. I've concluded that discovering our purpose is the foundation for living a satisfied life. This conclusion is nothing new, but its application certainly seems elusive to many working women, as evidenced by Anne's confession.

Over the years, I've conducted work-shops designed to help people of all ages and vocations uncover their purpose—CEOs, business owners, executives, and college students. All of them are eager to answer the question, *why*? However, most of them, like Anne, have spent little to no time thinking about it. Most people, myself included, spend time focused on the *what* of our lives.

> ## Discovering our purpose is the foundation for living a satisfied life.

What am I going to do with my life? What makes me happy? What do I want in a mate? What can I change to be more satisfied?

There are small distinctions between the words *why* and *what*. But the implications of answering these questions are vastly different. When put to our careers, answering *why* requires knowing our purpose. Webster's dictionary defines *purpose* this way: "a result or effect that is intended or desired; an intention."[4]

*What*, on the other hand, is answered by our mission—what it is we will do. *Mission* is defined as "a specific task with which a person or a group is charged."[5]

We first need to know why we are where we are, and why we want to do a particular thing, before we can decide what we will then do. In simple terms, we should know our motives before we lay out our mission.

The process of answering *why* is not that difficult. In fact, most of us already have a sense of the answer. We just don't take the time to think about it, ponder the elements that comprise it, and write something down so that our purpose is clear to ourselves and others.

Wouldn't you like to know why and to be able to answer for yourself and others, in a succinct manner, not only what you do but why you do it?

Envision yourself at a typical party or networking event. You strike up a conversation with someone who asks the usual question, "What do you do?" Rather than giving your job title, you instead tell the person why you do what you do. For me, it might go something like this: "I am passionate about helping people discover their purpose and live out their dreams. Speaking and writing are my favorite ways to do this."

Imagine the response. The individual has just been given a glimpse into my heart. He or she understands why I get out of bed in the morning. I bet it makes me more memorable, too, a woman with passion and purpose instead of only a name and job title.

**Wouldn't you like to be able to answer for yourself and others, in a succinct manner, not only what you do but why you do it?**

Now imagine that you and I are on my front porch and I ask you the all-important *why* question. Describe your deepest desire and dream. Then tell me why. Why do you want to do it? Why do you believe it will bring you fulfillment? The answers you share with me are clues to your purpose. They will help point your mind to the things your heart already knows.

On the pages that follow, you will find a more thorough exercise that should kick-start you along the path to clarifying your own personal purpose. It will get your juices flowing and help you write a personal purpose statement that captures the spirit of who you are and why you do what you do.

## ARTICULATING YOUR PURPOSE

Recently I was working with a group of executive women, women who have skillfully climbed the ladder to places of significant success and influence. Many of them are now asking what their next move should be. We ventured through this same exercise, which helped them think about their purpose. I loved looking across that room as these dear, brilliant women took time for themselves (something they rarely do) and thought about the bigger questions in life.

I asked them to circle words (like you will do in a minute) that spoke to them and excited them most. I then asked them to share with a partner why they chose those words. The room buzzed with excitement, laughter, and enthusiasm. The faces of these women brightened as they thought about what they love to do most and why.

Then they took the three or four descriptive words they circled and began putting them in a sentence to form their purpose statement. I told them to focus not on the flow of words but on getting the concepts together in a way that speaks of who they are.

Several of them shared their first stab at a purpose statement. Some of them had crafted statements that sounded eloquent, while others were still laboring to pull together phrases that hit the mark and made their hearts soar.

# Why Am I Working?

Bridgette Heller, president of the global baby and kids division of Johnson & Johnson, was one of these women. Not only did she write her purpose statement, but she shared with me a process of discovery she had gone through during the previous three years.

While vice president at Kraft Foods, she had enjoyed significant success. However, her daughters would soon be teenagers, and she needed to reassess her own definition of success.

I was now sitting at a place in corporate America that I never imagined I'd be, needing a definition of success that extended beyond where I was. So I began thinking about what was really important—a solid, happy family life, service to the community, and the personal/spiritual piece that is the foundation for everything else. I needed to define what success looked like in each of those realms.

The easier realms were family, community, and spiritual. The biggest struggle was the professional side. People will chart your progress and figure out if they are keeping up; they'll sabotage others. This had been draining and was inconsistent with my spiritual journey.

I came to grips with this as I decided to leave Kraft. I went through a grieving process, asking myself, "What am I doing walking away from everything I know to something I don't?" After three years of lots of soul-searching, I chose Johnson & Johnson.

My husband, chief of cardiology at a hospital in the Bronx at the time, watched how my soul searching brought me closer to our girls and gave me new clarity around what I wanted to do. It inspired him to quit cold turkey. Now it's his turn. He is taking classes and spending lots of time with our daughters, taking them on camping trips and having conversations that help them learn and grow.[6]

Our purpose is not something we can sit down and think about for a few minutes, then write with perfection. Rather, it's the start of a process to unlock our hearts, like Bridgette did. It is something that takes time, reflection, and thought.

Rarely do we give ourselves the chance to do this. We have a schedule to keep, kids to get to school, projects to finish, people to manage, planes to catch, e-mails to answer. But discovering our purpose is time well spent, time that sets the foundation for everything else we are hoping to receive or achieve.

There is something powerful about articulating truth. Have you ever heard someone describe something in a way that just perfectly captures a thought you've had or an idea you've pondered? You hear it phrased in just the right way, and you say, "Yes. That is what I've been feeling all along."

> Your purpose statement becomes, in many ways, your compass, guiding you to the activities, people, and places that will bring the deepest satisfaction and delight.

So it is with your purpose statement. It becomes the *aha* moment, that simple yet profound way of saying something that brings all the many facets of who you are and hope to be into focus. Your purpose statement becomes, in many ways, your compass, guiding you to the activities, people, and places that will bring the deepest satisfaction and delight.

The exercise that follows will coach you through a stimulating process of articulating your own purpose. It is a tool I have used for years with women of all ages and stages in their careers. The process is not rocket science and will only help you begin discovering and articulating answers to the whys of your life. But as you dive right in, this exercise will get your creative juices flowing in the right direction and help ignite new enthusiasm in your many endeavors.

## THE STRATEGY: CREATE A PURPOSE STATEMENT FOR LIFE AND WORK

Before you can articulate your purpose, you must first determine exactly what it is. Rarely is this a quick process or a one-time effort. Your purpose will evolve and change over time based on the season you are in and your level of self-knowledge.

Start by asking yourself the following questions:

## Why Am I Working?

1. When people explain why they want me involved or why they referred someone to me, what do they say?

2. Which of my abilities and gifts are most often noted and affirmed by my colleagues?

3. What activities bring me the most joy and satisfaction?

> **Your purpose will evolve and change over time based on the season you are in and your level of self-knowledge.**

4. What could I be passionate about doing for the next ten years?

5. If I could have any role/position at my current organization or elsewhere, what would I do?

6. Given my life experiences, my education, and my gifts, what unique attributes set me apart from others?

## Climbing the Ladder in Stilettos

Notice the adjectives and ideas in your answers above. Are there common threads? Do you see any words repeated in more than one answer? Do you find yourself going back to a consistent or central theme? If so, this is a good start toward defining your unique purpose. Keep these ideas in mind as we move now to your purpose statement.

Purpose statements usually include two elements:

- a word or phrase that indicates a change in status, such as *to increase, to decrease, to eliminate, to prevent*; and
- an identification of the problem or condition to be changed.

From the following list, circle the *four* words that most appeal to you. The words you choose will help you understand what actions most motivate and excite you.

| | | |
|---|---|---|
| Acquire | Counsel | Enlist |
| Advance | Create | Entertain |
| Affirm | Decrease | Enthuse |
| Alleviate | Deliver | Evaluate |
| Amplify | Demonstrate | Excite |
| Appreciate | Devise | Facilitate |
| Believe | Direct | Finance |
| Bestow | Discover | Foster |
| Brighten | Discuss | Further |
| Build | Distribute | Gather |
| Call | Draft | Generate |
| Combine | Dream | Give |
| Command | Drive | Grant |
| Communicate | Educate | Heal |
| Compel | Elect | Illuminate |
| Complete | Eliminate | Implement |
| Compliment | Embrace | Improve |
| Compose | Encourage | Inspire |
| Conceive | Endow | Integrate |
| Confirm | Engage | Involve |
| Connect | Engineer | Launch |
| Construct | Enhance | Lead |
| Continue | Enlighten | Make |

## Why Am I Working?

| | | |
|---|---|---|
| Mediate | Prevent | Safeguard |
| Model | Produce | Satisfy |
| Mold | Promote | Save |
| Motivate | Provide | Sell |
| Move | Reduce | Serve |
| Negotiate | Refine | Support |
| Nurture | Reform | Surrender |
| Open | Release | Sustain |
| Organize | Renew | Train |
| Persuade | Restore | Translate |
| Prepare | Return | Utilize |
| Present | Revise | Validate |

Look at the four words you selected. Why did you pick them? Are they similar to one another or different? You can keep all four or narrow them down even further.

Now, in the space below, using the words you have chosen, begin articulating your purpose statement. Write it out in a variety of ways. Then try to state your mission as well. Keep in mind that you are simply putting into language much of what you already know, and this is only a beginning point. Here is the simple outline to follow:

**My purpose is to:**

(WHY you do what you do—your purpose statement. Use the words you circled in the list above: *to increase, to build, to inspire, to bring,* etc.)

**Through or by or with:**

(WHAT you will do—your mission. This should be very general and include how you will impact others.)

As you write your purpose, let it "cook" for a while over the coming days and weeks. Ask your closest family members and friends if they think you're hitting

19

the mark. As new ideas emerge, feel free to write and rewrite them until you are happy with the result.

Remember that your purpose statement will change over time and be modified through the various seasons of your life. The central elements (the primary three or four words you selected), however, should remain fairly constant throughout your life and career.

**You should have one central purpose, but you may have many missions that accomplish that purpose.**

Don't forget the difference between purpose and mission. Focus on *why* you do what you do (purpose) versus *what* you want to do (mission). You should have one central purpose, but you may have many missions that accomplish that purpose.

As an example, my purpose is "to inspire and motivate people to live lives of hope, overcoming every challenge on the way to their dreams." This is a constant that weaves through my many missions. My missions are *what* I will do to achieve that purpose, and they are numerous—as a writer, a speaker, a wife and mother, a friend, and so forth.

So go ahead, write down ideas about your purpose and mission. Be bold. Dream out loud. Think big. Imagine what you would say in your proudest moment as you describe why your life matters and the difference you are making. Fear, guilt, or practicality may make you hesitant, but faith will keep you bold. Choose to believe in yourself, and resist fear during this significant time.

Having a concise purpose statement in writing puts you way out in front of most people and empowers you to keep on dreaming. Harvard psychologist David McClelland has extensively studied high achievers and concludes that successful people possess one common characteristic: they fantasize and dream incessantly about how to achieve their goals.[7]

Olympic downhill ski medalist and corporate speaker Bonnie St. John told me recently,

If you keep your vision [purpose] locked up inside and you never write it down, the odds of it actually happening are low. You need to be willing to talk about it. There are lots of reasons people don't want to talk about it, especially women. We can be perfectionists; we're afraid we're going to be seen as arrogant. So I say,

"You don't have to wait until your vision is perfect; if you do, you *will* sound arrogant." Rather, be in an open-ended conversation, saying, "This is what I'm thinking about doing. What do you think?"

If your talk is open-ended, it helps you clarify it and understand more about how to grow in it.[8]

Your purpose statement lays the foundation for your dreams and goals by helping you address the most important issue in life: knowing and understanding why you are here.

Once you get in tune with the whys of your career, then you can begin to answer the whats and hows. As we move throughout this book, we will build on this powerful foundation of purpose.

> **Once you get in tune with the whys of your career, then you can begin to answer the whats and hows.**

*We learn how to divorce our feelings in our work. . . . When you're alienated from yourself and others you don't understand what true intimacy is, how to dig deep inside yourself and recognize the feelings, acknowledging and valuing them, no matter how painful. We impoverish ourselves by not letting that happen. Discovering this truth has changed the whole texture of my life.*

—CECILY TRUETT
Sixteen-time Emmy-award-winning
producer of children's
television programs

# TWO

# These People Are Driving Me Crazy!

**O**f all the lessons I have learned in my career, there is one that I believe is more essential for success and satisfaction than any other.

It's a lesson many women I know have learned, and if you can grasp the same concepts and make them real for you, your success is going to be more rewarding and bring many more meaningful relationships than you ever imagined were possible. The concept I'm referring to is something I call *personal wholeness*.

Being *whole* is defined as

1. complete, including all parts or aspects, with nothing left out;
2. not damaged or broken;
3. not wounded, impaired, or incapacitated;
4. healed or restored to health physically or psychologically.[1]

When we are whole, we are complete, secure, and resilient in almost any circumstance. It is how we would describe a healthy person. On most days she feels great inside and out; she lives without chronic physical and emotional pain. She will occasionally get hurt, but she is healthy enough to heal and quickly bounce back. If she stubs her toe on the sofa leg, for instance, it is initially very painful. But because she has no other injuries, the pain soon goes away. Someone with personal wholeness is not impervious to pain or misfortune, but she is not lastingly affected by it.

> **When we are whole, we are complete, secure, and resilient in almost any circumstance.**

On the other hand, if she already has, say, a broken leg and then stubs her toe on the sofa, the agony that shoots up her body is almost unbearable. In fact, because she is already injured, any additional minor injury is potentially debilitating.

## THE CHALLENGE: I'M WORKING WITH BROKEN PEOPLE

It is not hard to recognize wounded people. Most display the following signs:

- are easily offended and carry offenses for a long time;
- are critical and talk negatively about themselves and others;
- have an insatiable need to be regularly affirmed and built up;
- refer often to themselves and their achievements, to the point of being embarrassing at times;
- react in illogical ways that produce anxiety in others;
- are easily angered;
- form social cliques and gossip about others;
- are overly consumed with taking care of everyone else, shutting down their own pain and focusing only on others; and
- use various addictions (cigarettes, alcohol, spending money) as a salve.

26

In contrast, people who are whole display the following signs:

- find it easy to affirm others and celebrate their successes;
- are not easily offended but offer grace when offenses do happen;
- bring comfort and encouragement to those around them;
- are goal-oriented, but their care for people always wins out over the bottom line;
- seek first to understand and then to be understood;
- are trusting, believing the best in others; and
- are modest and honest about their strengths and shortcomings.

Sadly, wholeness is not the typical state of most people we encounter in the workplace. Few of us grow up in healthy homes; we experience hurts and disappointments that lead to a brokenness that negatively affects our relationships. I suppose it is fair to say that in some ways, all of us are broken.

In an insightful article on the *Wall Street Journal*'s Career.com Web site, career counselor Cynthia Krainin describes what we often deal with at work:

> For most people, work is stressful due to productivity demands, deadlines, unpredictable bosses and constant change. This stress-filled environment can be viewed as a stage where family abuse and trauma events are re-enacted. It's the perfect place to reactivate old fears (e.g., making mistakes and paying for them later) and old reactions (e.g., feeling trapped when forced to work long hours), even though the time and circumstances are different.[2]

**Sadly, wholeness is not the typical state of most people we encounter in the workplace.**

An interesting example of the power of personal wholeness happened several years ago for me, via an e-mail exchange. I sent an e-mail requesting some data from a woman who provided many reports to numerous people throughout our company. We were not close friends but had a friendly working relationship. My request was not unusual, and I asked her very cordially, with no expectation of receiving the information immediately.

When she responded to my e-mail request, rather than clicking Forward, she hit Reply. So I received the response that she had intended for someone else. In her reply, she implied that my request was unrealistic and suggested I was "grandstanding" to make points with my bosses. She then suggested that the intended recipient call my two bosses (whom I referenced in my e-mail) and see what they "really wanted," thus avoiding me altogether.

I was sitting at my desk reading this e-mail, initially thinking it was her reply to me. I must have read it three or four times, trying to understand it, before I realized it was never intended for my eyes at all.

Once I grasped what had happened, I was fuming, utterly offended that she had the nerve to assume I was grandstanding. I was furious that she suggested going around my back to my bosses, making me look inept in their eyes. I wanted to hit Reply and send a seething e-mail right back to her. I pictured her sitting there mortified at the realization of what she had done.

Then I remembered I had committed myself to being an agent of wholeness, someone others could trust and knew cared about them. I decided instead to craft an e-mail that went like this (names have been changed):

Pam,

I think you mistakenly sent this e-mail to me. I'm sure you are under a lot of pressure and that my request may have seemed inappropriate. Tom and Mike did indeed request this information, and I was not grandstanding but rather just trying to accommodate their request, realizing that you are the best source for the information they need. I would appreciate a chance to discuss how to get this information for them in a time frame that works for you.

Thanks so much,
Lynette

I was nervous when I hit Send. The exchange felt awkward, but I knew I had responded in a way that I would have wanted her to if I was in her shoes (which I have been).

Not five minutes later she was at my door, apologetic and embarrassed.

"Lynette, I am *very sorry*. I never should have sent that e-mail. I am under some major deadlines with the top leaders, and I'm not handling the pressure very well. I am so, so sorry for this."

"It's no problem at all," I responded. "I really do understand, and I've been there myself, believe me." We talked a bit more, and from that day forward our relationship was stronger. Though we did not often work closely together, when we did there were mutual respect and appreciation between us. What a lesson that was for me.

## HURTING PEOPLE HURT PEOPLE . . . BUT RARELY INTEND TO

This interaction with my colleague reminded me that difficult people rarely want to be difficult. And when we choose not to be easily offended, when we take the time to understand or give others the benefit of the doubt, it opens up all kinds of doors and builds respect and trust between us.

Having told you that story, I don't want to imply that I am some sort of an angel at work. This example is overall a positive one, but sadly, there have been many times when I reacted much differently. For years, I was far more broken than I realized.

My journey toward personal wholeness began when I was a junior in college, having just turned twenty-one. I was fighting discouragement about my weight. I had put on the "freshmen ten" in the first ten weeks of school. The extra ten pounds grew to twenty over the next two years, and loving clothes and fashion like I do, it was exasperating and depressing to try desperately to lose the weight with no success.

> When we choose not to be easily offended, it opens up all kinds of doors and builds respect and trust between us.

Every night I would stand in front of the mirror after washing the makeup off my face, tears streaming down my cheeks. Those cheeks and my upper neck were covered with cystic acne. I had been to several dermatologists and tried every remedy possible, but the condition remained. I felt fat and ugly.

Amid this pain, my junior year I was selected to serve as a resident adviser. It was a fulfilling role, but it became one pressure too many. I was in tears much of the time with an increasing sense that I simply could not cope. I felt constantly pressured by a strong need to be excellent and perfect and beautiful, to be what all the girls on the floor needed, to be a great student, a true friend, and the right kind of faithful daughter and sister.

I talked to my parents at length during those months, trying to understand why I couldn't seem to cope. They suggested I see a therapist to sort through the that might be causing the stress. Since my parents had gone to counseling early in their marriage and received tremendous help, I took their advice. I checked out of the dorm for two weeks and began meeting with a therapist at the counseling center on campus.

> The process of getting honest with our own pain and hurts, acknowledging the wrongs done to us, and admitting our own mistakes begins to forge a path to personal wholeness.

Over the next six weeks, we peeled away layers to get to the root issues of my anxiety and pain. The counselor got me talking about my parents and my upbringing. I considered my parents to be role models, nearly perfect in their parenting, and my home a stable and favorite place to be. What I didn't realize is that I'd been missing a crucial element in my emotional development.

My dad was a strong man of character and integrity, our "steady Eddie" in a house of three women. But my dad wasn't an expressive man. I don't remember him ever telling me he loved me, hugging me, or kissing me.

Up to that point I had never considered that my dad's lack of expression had caused unhappiness or pain. I knew he loved me. He spent time with my sister and me, advising us and talking to us. We shared dinners as a family. We laughed together in front of the TV.

But the truth was, although I sensed that my dad loved me, he never showed that affection directly. Every girl needs a daddy who holds her and lavishes her with words of love and affection. Mine hadn't, and I thought I was fine.

As the counselor and I continued this conversation, I began to realize I was compensating for a lack of emotional nurturing through my various attempts to be perfect. I had subconsciously concluded that if I was perfect, my dad would finally tell me he loved me and was proud of me. I was crying out for my father's approval. This was a right and appropriate need, and I had to acknowledge that it was a legitimate void.

Becoming a resident adviser and having to please the thirty young women in my dorm was finally the one thing more than I could handle. It pushed me over the edge and headlong into the void.

As anyone who has ever gone through effective counseling knows, coming to the truth brings a freedom like never before. Suddenly so much made sense to me. I could see my harmful patterns of behavior and the toll they took on me and others.

The process of getting honest with our own pain and hurts, acknowledging the wrongs done to us, and admitting our own mistakes begins to forge a path to personal wholeness. The path is necessary not only for our personal lives but also for our professional lives, which unendingly intersect the lives of others.

## LEARNING NEW PATTERNS

It is as if we each have a tape recorder in our heads. The tape needs to be filled with words of love and nurturing from early on in our lives. Like me, many of us have sections of blank tape—places where words were needed yet no words were given. Others have the wrong messages on their tapes—lies harshly spoken or words of destruction and ruin. Over and over these tapes run through our minds, often without our knowledge or resistance.

After my sessions with the counselor, I spent the next several years filling my tape with truth about a woman's worth, about how beauty comes from the inside and not the outside, recognizing that my value is in *who I am* more than in *what I do*. I spent hours writing in my journals the words I

> I began retraining myself to think and respond in a healthy manner. As I did, I began to experience a freedom and joy I'd never known before.

had longed all my life to hear from my dad. The identity I derive from my faith became an important component of my healing as well. As I did all of this, the blank sections on my tape were being filled. I was on the path to wholeness.

Occasionally, when I'd notice the perfectionism kicking in again, I'd stop and check my motives. I began retraining myself to think and respond in a healthy manner. As I did these things, I began to experience a freedom and joy I'd never known before. Eventually, I could steer others down a similar path.

Personal wholeness is available and essential for everyone, but so few stay on the path necessary to find it. Russian novelist Leo Tolstoy was right when he wrote, "Everyone thinks of changing the world but no one thinks of changing himself." While this is not a self-help book on brokenness and the need for healing, I would be remiss not to spend a chapter on how the subject affects our work lives. I have observed and experienced many difficulties in the workplace that I believe stem from a general lack of wholeness in so many individuals.

This observation makes better sense when we consider that in 2004, the Department of Health and Human Services estimated that the annual incidence of abuse and neglect of children is likely around nine million cases.[3] To add to this, the National Association of Children of Alcoholics estimates that one in every five people is raised in an alcoholic family.[4]

These estimates suggest that in any workplace of at least twenty people, between three and five are likely to have experienced abuse or neglect as a child. The numbers are even higher when considering those from alcohol-impacted families.

Since we spend the vast majority of our time and energy at work, we can reasonably deduce that our broken patterns of relating will be strewn throughout the workplace. Cynthia Krainin explains it this way:

> The link between childhood and work impacts everyone, regardless of whether they've experienced abuse. Each of us brings personal issues to work, no matter how healthy we are. We carry our parents' life experiences, expectations and failures. Some people struggle with success simply because their parents did. Everyone is affected by their primary caretakers in a way that impacts self-esteem and how they perceive themselves at work.[5]

It would be nice if we could keep our baggage private. But that's like keeping a broken leg hidden at the office, thinking we can just paint the cast the color of our skin and convince everyone that the limp is nothing new.

Think about the people with whom you work on a regular basis. Don't many of them display areas of brokenness? Consider the symptoms outlined at the beginning of this chapter. How much easier would it be if your coworkers didn't carry such anger? Weren't so depressed or stressed? Quit being negative or critical about themselves and the rest of the team? Had joy and a consistency of belief in human potential? Were resilient and offered comfort and grace to their colleagues?

How much easier would it be if all these things were true of you?

## THE STRATEGY: BECOME PERSONALLY WHOLE

While we cannot heal our coworkers, we can change how we treat brokenness. In turn, this will change how others relate to us.

As healed and emotionally healthy individuals, we can be resilient—even encouraging—when encountering those who are broken. But to do this, we must understand what went wrong in our own lives and why, fill the blank sections of our internal tapes, and then train ourselves how to operate in healthy ways. We will soon begin to see real, sustainable transformation in our relationships and in our work environments.

> As healed and emotionally healthy individuals, we can be resilient—even encouraging—when encountering those who are broken.

My friend Cecily Truett is a sixteen-time Emmy winner and recipient of numerous Peabody awards. Along with her husband and partner, Larry Lancit, she built a hugely successful production company that brought children's programming like *Reading Rainbow* to television for twenty-five years. She and I were catching up recently, and I was inspired as she described her journey toward personal wholeness over the last couple of years.

I did a great job of serving everyone else's children. It was a mission and passion, but in a sense it was also a distraction from the intimacy that I needed but didn't know how to achieve with those who mattered most. In some ways it was easier to be passionate about children I didn't know. The sense of reward, mission, and purpose in my work was true, noble, and good. It brought a great deal of fulfillment. But I wish I had known the rewards that could have been reaped by all of us had I been more aware of service and intimacy with my children and

33

husband. My great learning experience in life has come from understanding that now.

I was fifty when we sold the company. I floundered looking for a new mission for three or four years. Then through a crisis with one of our daughters I found a therapist. She brought tremendous healing to my entire family. She helped me find my new mission, a transition that was a very frightening and scary one for me. I went from a mission that was huge, worldly, big, and wonderful to one that was deep, personal, and intimate—learning how to be a loving person one-on-one with the people who were most important in my life.

If I could go back, I would set greater limits on my commitment—my addiction and passion for my work—and redirect it toward my children and family. I did not neglect them; they were loved and had a warm, loving family. But a missing piece was "serving them." That is a mission too.

We learn how to divorce our feelings in our work. Finding that connectedness is something my therapist helped me discover. I had no idea there are ways to grow, to seek these things out. When you're alienated from yourself and others, you don't understand what true intimacy is, how to dig deep inside yourself and recognize the feelings, acknowledging and valuing them, no matter how painful. We impoverish ourselves by not letting that happen. Discovering this truth has changed the whole texture of my life. I have been an extremely private person. The fact that I would tell this story is part of my evolution.[6]

My friend's story is not uncommon in the world of working women. I encounter similar stories on a regular basis. According to Mary Bellofatto, a licensed mental health therapist in Naples, Florida—a city full of dynamic, highly successful women—the issue of not accessing true intimacy is one many working women unknowingly face. Bellofatto points to the mistaken substitutions so many women like Cecily make for true intimacy.

Women today are under tremendous pressure. Not only are they pushing to be more than their mothers (while they honor what their mothers represented, they say it's not enough). They've now taken on the role of their dads as well—working to succeed at home *and* succeed at work, make money, have both parallel lives happening at once—be like Mom and Dad all wrapped up in one role. We see women sacrificing the connections of their inner soul. While striving for things—clothes, a certain look, a way of being—they have lost that internal peace with themselves.[7]

Whether we suffer from intimacy issues or another type of brokenness, dealing with the root causes is our first step to personal wholeness. Once we've forged the path, we are then able to become what I call agents of wholeness in our workplaces. This role is one of the most fulfilling we can aspire to in our careers. It will rewrite the memories we create, the relationships we form, and the eventual impact of our many endeavors.

## STEPS TO PERSONAL WHOLENESS

There are several practical ways that we can begin reaping the rewards of personal wholeness. The following four embody the approach many working women I know have successfully taken over the years.

*Start with yourself.* Take an honest look at your life and relationships. Are you basically a healthy, whole person? Would your friends and family agree? If you see symptoms of brokenness in yourself, don't ignore them. Admit your brokenness and take steps to deal with it. Rather than adjust your entire life around the broken leg, go in for "surgery." The surgery will have a price: time and emotional energy, potentially some relational mending. It might get messy.

> There is no denying that the journey to personal wholeness is a risk— but, oh, is the potential reward worth it.

This messiness is what turns most women off. Who has the time? Who has the patience or the stamina? So much in our lives is already emotionally charged; why seek out more trauma?

There is no denying that the journey to personal wholeness is a risk—but, oh, is the potential reward worth it. Once the broken leg is healed, not only can you walk normally again, but you can run, leap, skip, and climb. Most important, you can lead others down a similar path.

Mary Bellofatto explains this well.

Say hello to the pain, embrace it, then move beyond it. You don't have to get in it and spend the rest of your life there. Therapy works best for those who will get in and get their issues dealt with, then move forward. You come in for short spurts, work on issues, go out and put it into practice, come back and deal with another piece if necessary. Allow the pain to bring into your life resiliency. Conflict is growth trying to happen. When there is conflict, get excited; find your solution. Ask, "What is the higher message and higher good here?"[8]

*Become an agent of wholeness.* As a whole person, you will have new levels of compassion and understanding. Your wounds will no longer drain you of the ability to look beyond yourself. You will see others through a lens that reveals deeper, nonthreatening reasons people do the things they do. You will see beyond their behaviors and develop the capacity to show mercy instead of judgment.

I had a gratifying experience with this several years ago. The man I was working for at the time had some obvious brokenness issues and was very insecure. His workdays were spent trying to make his own way, and he therefore had little interest in supporting any of us on his team. For months I was disappointed and aggravated with him, exasperated at times. I saw him as my primary roadblock to meeting goals, and although he had likable traits, I could hardly stand to work around his insatiable thirst for validation.

One day it finally hit me. Instead of being resistant to him and agitated by his behavior, perhaps I could help. I started considering the part of his personal life that I knew was painful, struggles I imagined he was still having at home. With this new perspective, I became less critical and more compassionate. It was easier to be patient with him when I remembered how painful his home life was. I started listening to him more often and encouraging him on the various endeavors our team was pursuing. I could see his countenance lift each time we chatted. Eventually, I knew that he could sense I was for him, unlike most of the others.

Over time, he became one of my strongest advocates and was the catalyst for a promotion I had been wanting for a long time. Though this wasn't the reason I decided to help him, it was in forging my own path to personal wholeness that I began to see him in a new light. This new perspective impacted not only his career but mine too.

*Speak only positive things about others.* The Golden Rule is as effective today as it was thousands of years ago: "Treat others the way you would want them to treat you." If we have a habit of belittling or criticizing others, it may take time to retrain ourselves to hold our tongues when the opportunity to speak negatively arises. Mastering this skill took me some time, but the rewards have been wonderful.

A man I worked for several years ago, a key leader and role model of a significant group in our company, had a horrible habit of talking about others behind their backs. Many people do this occasionally, but he was the worst I'd ever seen! Virtually every time I met with him, he would speak negatively about someone. While there were times when it was tempting (and much safer) to agree with him, I continually fought to keep my mouth shut.

His behavior became increasingly unacceptable in my view. I wanted to slip under his office door every article I could find on why belittling others is a death wish for any leader. Instead, the only choice I felt I had was to simply avoid entering into the discussion. I would listen and sometimes mention something positive about the person, bringing up a possibility that gave them the benefit of the doubt.

I'll never forget one day, after about a year of this practice, I was in a meeting with this man and a few others. They were all going on and on about someone negatively and then looked to me to chime in.

At that moment, the leader piped up. "Oh, Lynette will never say anything negative about anyone." He said it in a teasing way, but I could sense respect in his voice. I was grateful and equally embarrassed, but the exchange was a great reminder that the choice I had made was noticed. I assumed the man never gave thought to it, but my small decision apparently made an impression on him.

While I don't remember him ever changing his ways, I found satisfaction in sticking to my guns, sometimes to the potential detriment of my job. It was worth it.

*See your workplace as a practice field for greatness.* It is easy to fall into a rut. We do the same job over and over, talk to the same people about the same things, and follow predictable patterns of relating. There are those we like and those we don't. It may feel awkward or seem impossible to break out of these patterns and bring change. But if you do, you will feel new energy and life coming into your work. People will look to you as a leader and not just one of the pack. Whole people in the workplace are so rare that if you become one, you will be amazed at how many opportunities open up for you as people recognize that you bring people together instead of tearing them down or apart.

> Whole people in the workplace are so rare that if you become one, you will be amazed at how many opportunities open up for you to.

It will often feel like a risk, but great people are familiar with taking risks. JFK was right when he said, "There are risks and costs to a program of action. But they are far less than the long-range risks and costs of comfortable inaction."

These simple yet powerful steps to personal wholeness will yield so much positive energy that you will be amazed. New patterns built on wholeness bring life and encouragement to the workplace.

I'm certainly not a perfect agent of personal wholeness, but my aim is to become someone who is patient and understanding, who is utterly trustworthy, and who cares much more about people than about processes or results. Someone who believes in potential and possibilities, who cheers others on to become all they are meant to be.

Won't you join me? Just imagine what a difference we can make and how much more fulfilling and satisfying our workplaces will be when whole, healed people take the lead in building environments where people at work really want to be.

*My mother raised me to think of others before myself, and I've tried to raise my daughters to be the same way. . . . But now I notice that my sixteen-year-old, who is passionate about community service and has risen to positions of leadership in her extracurricular activities, is spending a lot of her time making sure that everyone else has what they need. . . . So I said to her, "You need to be more selfish with your time. . . ." the irony of the mixed message wasn't lost on me. After telling her to be unselfish all these years, now I was suddenly asking her to be more selfish.*

—ANDREA BAUMANN LUSTIG
Investment management adviser

# THREE

# No One Appreciates
# Me Around Here!

W hen was the last time you heard any of the following from someone at work?

- You are such a gift to this organization!
- Your abilities and talents make such a huge difference for everyone here!
- What would we do without your energy and investments?
- What can I do to show you how valuable you are to me and to our team?

I haven't heard these kinds of statements very often. I imagine you haven't either. Why are appreciation, recognition, and reward such rare commodities in our professional lives?

Starting a career in my early twenties, I was just sure that if I found something I was passionate about, liked the people I was working for, and worked for a company that had a reputation for treating people well, not only would I

41

be highly valued and rewarded, but I would *feel* it most of the time.

I woke up ten years later and realized that the opposite was more accurate. I had an overriding, general sense of disappointment. Not the despairing kind. Not one that rendered me helpless, bitter, or confused. It was just a subtle sense of gnawing. A sense that amid whatever success I might have achieved thus far, somehow I'd missed something important and even deserved.

I wanted to feel more utilized, that my abilities were better woven into my work. And what about my gifts for decorating and fashion, my interests in the arts and nutrition—couldn't they also be somehow incorporated into the work in which I invested my most creative waking hours? I longed to be sincerely appreciated and recognized for my efforts and the energy that I invested so liberally each hour of the business day (and oftentimes for hours after leaving the office).

Then there was the issue of salary. Working for a nonprofit organization at the time, I was well aware that I was not likely to become wealthy, especially with the financial challenges my employer was enduring at the time. The stress of living on so little for so long often took its toll, especially when a friend called to tell me she and her husband had just closed on their second home while I was still living in my first little apartment.

There have been occasional moments since then when I have felt appreciated, if not always by my boss, then certainly by the people I have served. There have also been times when I felt as though the majority of my skills were being utilized and that I was recognized in ways that were satisfying. For some reason, though, I assumed these feelings would be present much more often and more deeply than they have been.

## THE CHALLENGE: I'M UNDERUTILIZED, UNRECOGNIZED, AND UNDERPAID

Many of the working women I talk to feel the same way much of the time. We wish we were recognized by others, deeply appreciated in ways that mean something to us, rewarded not just fairly but liberally, and allowed to flourish in all of our many abilities and talents. Often that's just not the case.

An interesting study conducted by Towers Perrin and Gang & Gang indicates these same desires exist across the board for most employees. Their research shows that people relate to work on a very strong, personal level, yet overall emotions about their current work experience are decidedly negative.

Additionally, the study found that people tend to define their total work experience in three "my" categories:

> **People relate to work on a very strong, personal level, yet overall emotions about their current work experience are decidedly negative.**

1. *Myself*—the extent to which work gives me a sense of confidence, competence, and control over my destiny
2. *My job*—the nature of what I do, how I contribute, how I'm recognized and rewarded
3. *My workplace*—the people I work with and for, the company's culture and atmosphere[1]

While we may agree that having personalized expectations in these categories is just and fair, sometimes our expectations produce an awkward tension. We aren't always sure about this concept of deserving. Shouldn't we just be content with serving? Isn't there some reward for laboring in secret, serving others without expectation, simply being grateful for what we are given and what we can give?

Maybe we get these ideas from our mothers and grandmothers. Women have historically been in positions of service, often underpaid if paid at all, called upon to sacrifice for the good of others. We grow up being told to think of others over ourselves. It is better to give than to receive. Don't seek your own accolades. And so forth.

### HOW MUCH SHOULD WE SERVE?

My friend Andrea Baumann Lustig, a highly accomplished financial adviser who worked for years as a management consultant and on Wall Street, shared with me recently how she sees this tendency toward sacrificial service already showing up in her daughter. She also acknowledged the tension it creates.

> My mother raised me to think of others before myself, and I've tried to raise my
> daughters to be the same way. They're getting all the messages that a liberal soci-

ety would want them to have. But now I notice that my sixteen-year-old, who is passionate about community service and has risen to positions of leadership in her extracurricular activities, is spending a lot of her time making sure that everyone else has what they need and not starting her homework until after she's taken care of everything else. So I said to her, "You need to be more selfish with your time—do your own homework first for your personal grade before you serve all these other people." The irony of the mixed message wasn't lost on me. After telling her to be unselfish all these years, now I was suddenly asking her to be more selfish.

I could see it didn't make sense to her, and it didn't feel right to me either. I want her to be generous, but I don't want her to lose opportunities because she doesn't pay enough attention to herself. It wasn't until I used the same word with my trainer that the proverbial light bulb went off.

I had admitted to the trainer that I just wasn't being selfish enough to find the time to work out and take care of myself. She told me that *selfish* was the wrong word. I needed to be more *devoted* to myself. Bingo! I went in to my daughter that night and suggested that she needed to be just as devoted to her own dreams and her needs as she was to helping others.

It seems to me that the most successful women executives have internalized both these messages and are therefore better able to focus on developing the skills and networks they themselves need to climb the ladder. They may be devoted to their careers, but they are also devoted to themselves.[2]

I can relate to her daughter's dilemma. Perhaps we all can.

Serving is the highest form of our work. When we serve others through our jobs, we give people something that is more significant than an end product. Historically, serving others is something that women seem to have a natural capacity for doing.

Betty Lehan Harragan's classic book *Games Mother Never Taught You* further illustrates this point. It was written in the 1970s but has some interesting insights that are relevant still today. She describes how women often have the impression that the business team is a fluid group all working together, each person doing whatever they do best, fulfilling any duty that needs doing at the moment—in other words, serving the good of the team at the possible expense of themselves. Harragan says this is a mistake.

"Good team members," she explains, "are counted on to handle their specific responsibilities, and that's all. No ballplayer runs all over the field playing assorted positions; the rules are very strict about that. But every team member is expected to do whatever job is assigned and do it as well as possible. Young women players are most guilty of violating this latter injunction and wonder later why they can't get promoted to better jobs."[3] In other words, our internal messages may not always help us, though no one is arguing that service to the team or the greater good is not a worthwhile practice.

## IS RECOGNITION OVERRATED?

Many of our role models have also been dedicated to serving others. One of the women I discovered in grade school was Clara Barton. Founder of the American Red Cross, she worked as a nurse in the Civil War and lived her entire life serving others before dying at the age of ninety (which was quite an accomplishment back in the early 1900s).

I also loved Harriet Tubman, a runaway slave from Maryland who became known as the Moses of her people. I found it fascinating how she led hundreds of slaves to freedom along the Underground Railroad, a secret network of safe houses where runaway slaves could stay on their journey to freedom in the North. During the Civil War, she was a spy for the federal forces in South Carolina as well as a nurse. I marveled then and now at her personal courage and sacrifice.

These women, and so many others like them, worked for little or nothing. Their paychecks were small or nonexistent, their rewards and recognition not fully acknowledged at the time, if ever. And even in my mother's generation, most women who worked became nurses or teachers, worthy professions of service and, still today, professions largely comprised of women.

Granted, we working women in general have made tremendous strides in the last twenty years, entering virtually every profession, earning better and better pay, given privileges and opportunities that our grandmothers only dreamed of having. So shouldn't we just be grateful?

Yes and no. We can be grateful, yes, but we can still acknowledge the legitimate desire to feel truly recognized and rewarded for all we give, do, and achieve.

## WHAT ABOUT MY DREAMS?

Early in my career, I worked at a university. It was my second job out of college, serving as assistant alumni director at my alma mater in Oklahoma. When I was

45

interviewing for the job, they explained that I would come in as assistant director, spend a year or two in that role learning the ropes, and then be promoted to alumni director. The plan sounded good, and I was willing to take a pay cut to dive into this new, exciting role.

About eighteen months into it, as I was still waiting for the promotion and the promised pay raise, the current alumni director resigned after seventeen years at the university. She had become a dear friend and a great professional mentor. While I hated to see her go, I figured now would be the obvious time for me to be promoted to her position. Sadly, another man was appointed.

I found it tough to get out of bed some mornings but chose to be optimistic that very soon things would turn around in my favor. My new boss also became a dear friend, and since he initially knew little about the alumni programs, I, in many respects, served as the director while he grew into his new role.

The university was enduring major financial challenges at the time. Our budgets were cut and cut again. We had only a couple of faithful staff members in our department, along with several student workers. We spent hours on the phone and in person, appealing to alumni to believe in the vision and to get involved in helping us build and grow.

Those were in many ways rewarding times, yet I often fought discouragement. While my friends were getting raises, buying homes, putting money in 401(k) accounts, and having children, I was plugging away on my small salary, wondering if I'd ever have a savings account, waiting for a promotion and raise. I found myself asking lots of questions and fielding lots of frustrations.

> We can be grateful, yes. But we can still acknowledge the legitimate desire to feel truly recognized and rewarded.

*What about all my visions and dreams? Here I am in this relatively insignificant role, with no staff, no money to work with, no one to mentor and train me. I don't know what I'm doing half the time. When will my season of flourishing come?*

Instead of eighteen months, it was about eight years into my tenure when the promised promotion came. I was finally named the director for alumni and public relations. Along with the new title came an increase in my salary. That, along with praise from my coworkers and notes of congratulation from the alumni whom I'd long served, made me feel fully appreciated and compensated for the first time in years.

Too bad those feelings didn't last very long. They might have lingered six months. Even in those first months following the promotion, there were moments when I questioned whether things were what they should be, whether they were what I had waited for so long. Did I deserve more? Was I being ungrateful? Were my expectations unrealistic?

## WHAT WE DESERVE

Isn't that how it often goes? We labor long for that promotion. Play the political games; please those who need pleasing. Give up personal time. Sacrifice our health in some cases; burn out and press on. Once in a while, someone notices. We appreciate their recognition but want to scream, "Show me the money!" or "Tell it to my boss and ask her to act on it this time!"

I've often wondered what it would be like to work for someone who is proactive on my behalf. I have looked around to see whether I could identify someone, anyone, who exemplified this talent in leadership. After all, being proactive is a basic leadership skill, isn't it?

The people I have worked for certainly, at times, displayed this attribute in small degrees or at opportune moments, for which I was grateful and invigorated. Still, my job satisfaction has often been low and my overall frustration high. It's easy to tell ourselves that we should be grateful to have a job and should appreciate what we've been given. Maybe we just need to quit being so idealistic about our boss or colleagues or career and not be so needy for approval and appreciation.

Over the years, I've learned to reduce my expectations and, thus, my disappointments. These feelings now only seem to emerge when I *expect* to be rewarded, following a glowing midyear review, for example, or when annual compensation increases are given and I know I added tremendous value to the company. Nevertheless, I've found a few very positive ways to deal proactively with these needs and feelings.

Somewhere along the way, I recognized that what I wanted from my boss was unlikely to come. So I began to develop several personal strategies that have helped me stay encouraged along the path. They have also helped me discover new creative outlets beyond a list of requirements and job responsibilities.

## THE STRATEGY: ADOPT METHODS
## FOR GAINING NEW JOY AND SATISFACTION

The strategies I developed address the categories that typically have a positive impact on our emotions about work:

- *Sense of self-worth*—the extent to which my job makes me feel competent, confident, worthwhile, and in control

- *Results*—the contribution I can make to my company and work team

- *People*—the individuals I work with and the quality of my relationships with them

As I share these strategies, consider your current situation or status in each of the following categories.

### WHEN YOU FEEL UNDERUTILIZED

When I have the sense of my job description being too narrowly defined or when I have wondered if the company would allow me to expand my responsibilities, I have done one of two things—either I look beyond my job description, or I find new ways to work within it.

*Look beyond the job description.* Back when I was acting as alumni director at the university for quite some time without the title, I was somewhat bored with the responsibilities. I had been in the role for several years and needed something more.

My interest in public relations was strongly emerging, and I began to think about how to get more connected in the community. At the time, I was getting to know two corporate real estate brokers who were helping the university lease its hospital complex. They, in turn, had introduced me to a man who was leasing and managing an expanding shopping complex on an adjacent corner.

One day the idea hit me that perhaps we could all benefit from meeting together periodically and talking about development ideas for our growing corner of the city. My broker friends thought the idea had merit, so we scouted out the top leaders of three other major businesses at 81st Street and Lewis Avenue, and we called our first lunch meeting.

One of the participants offered to host the meeting, and another offered to cater lunch. Along with one of my broker friends, I put together an agenda and hosted the luncheon, which, after two hours, was deemed a success by all who attended.

We decided to make it a monthly gathering and within two months had named ourselves "The 81st and Lewis Alliance." We had our photo and a write-up in the paper outlining our members and our vision for community growth in our small corner of the world. I began to be a recognized leader of the group, and my personal fulfillment soared. I enjoyed my new relationships outside the university and loved being able to explore new challenges and talents.

I did not know what I was doing when I began. I didn't decide, "I'm going to organize a community corporate alliance group." I just knew I wanted to meet new people and broaden my experience, so I built on relationships with a couple of people I considered movers and shakers and decided to simply give it a try. It proved to be a hugely significant move in my career and a tremendous lesson.

The experience illustrates a point that Cathy Benko, the national managing director of Deloitte's Women's Initiative, shared with me. I asked her what one thing she would share with a younger woman, a lesson she has learned on her path to success. "Don't wait for someone to give you permission," she said. "Simply assume that you have it, and use it wisely, though not necessarily sparingly."[4]

I love that principle and share it often in workshops, asking women if they ever feel they need to wait for permission to do something. Heads nod all over the room. It seems that many of us as women don't want to seem too aggressive or presumptuous, so we wait for an invitation or approval to try something new.

> **The difference between those who do and those who don't is that those who do, simply do.**

One of my personal mottos is this: The difference between those who do and those who don't is that those who do, simply do. So why not do whatever it is that you really want to do? Right now, today, without formal permission or an official job description or title. Do what is in your heart, the things that will add new fulfillment and joy to your work, things that align with your purpose.

If you're young, keep in mind a point the great Nobel laureate Richard Feynman made. It is no coincidence, he explained, that virtually all major discoveries in physics have been made by those under the age of twenty-five, because when you're under twenty-five, you don't know what you don't know.[5]

If you didn't complete the exercise in chapter 1 on writing a concise purpose statement, I encourage you to do it now. Write your purpose statement, understand why you do what you do, and then ask, "Why not? Why not me, why not now, why not these few things that could bring significant new zest and fulfillment to this job now?" If you do this, you will be amazed at how one idea or experiment can bring increased energy and enthusiasm to your everyday work.

> Put the concept of *change* out of your mind for now, and start thinking about *addition*.

Think for a few minutes, or maybe over the next couple of weeks, about how you can expand your role without being asked to or given permission. Put the concept of *change* out of your mind for now, and start thinking about *addition*.

- What skills do you possess now or want to cultivate that are not being utilized in your current work?
- In what creative ways can you carry out your current responsibilities using these skills?
- What knowledge do you gain, perhaps from even the most mundane tasks you perform, that could equip you to expand your role?

*Add new perspective to the work you are already doing.* By stepping back from your tasks and looking at them through the lens of the role you really want to have, you can likely find ways to make your current work connect you to broader opportunities.

For example, while I was working at Deloitte, several of the junior marketing associates detested their responsibility of keying in financial data from our major global clients. These were tedious monthly reports that showed the sales in the pipeline for each account team. From their perspective, the task seemed completely unrelated to their marketing role, and in truth, it was.

I encouraged them to begin spending time reading the data and analyzing it in the context of which projects were selling and why. The simple addition of analysis could help them become some of the most informed people on the team. They could then come to meetings not merely to remind people to submit their data but also to offer important insights they gained from their analysis of the data. This positioned them as strategists, a role they wanted but didn't feel they had with the title of associate.

Other questions to ask yourself if you feel underutilized include these:

- Does your work connect you to people whom you have not taken full advantage of for networking, mentoring, and rewarding connections?
- Are there any projects on the horizon you could volunteer to be part of in order to meet new people and add to your knowledge bank?
- Are there associations or membership organizations that you could become part of, even on your personal time, that would broaden your knowledge and relationships while expanding your opportunities?

I was talking with my sister recently about a situation in which she felt limited and somewhat helpless. She put the situation into perfect perspective. "Instead of saying I'm *trapped*," she explained, "I'm going to say I'm *planted*." I love that point of view. It changes everything. Instead of playing the victim, I'm in a position to grow, to spread roots, and to drink in the elements I need to thrive right here and right now. My sister has done this well, and her life is more beautiful and hopeful because of it. Yours will be too.

Westina Matthews Shatteen, managing director of community leadership at Merrill Lynch in New York, shared with me a principle she uses in her life that sums up well what we are discussing.

Every year I try to take on something I wouldn't normally think I could do. Last year my husband gave me a bicycle, so I took my bike and rode around our neighborhood. It was so hard, a fifty-something woman on a bike, but I did it. Then last fall I got my driver's license for the first time in many, many years. I decided it was time to drive again, so I went back to driving school and took driving lessons. My palms were sweating and I was shaking, but I saw again how when we get outside of our comfort zones and take a risk, there are so many roads that open up. The bike and car were metaphors for me for opening up new roads ahead. When I began doing both, I was heading for places I couldn't even imagine going.[6]

## WHEN YOU FEEL UNRECOGNIZED

If you feel that your boss or those around you are not fully recognizing your talents and abilities, then the first thing to do is let go of the belief that their recognition is crucial to your advancement.

This lesson has been a hard one for me to learn. My inner sense of justice is offended when I work hard and go the extra mile time and again, yet the person I work for, who personally gains the most from my commitment, does not seem to recognize my impact.

So when I grow impatient, discouraged, and frustrated with the seemingly slow path to promotion or lack of recognition that my work brings, I choose to remember the Clara Bartons and Harriet Tubmans of the world—women who had no job description or performance bonuses yet chose to follow their purpose and passion nonetheless.

I am inspired by this quote from Helen Keller, who was blind and deaf from birth: "Character cannot be developed in ease and quiet. Only through experience of trial and suffering can the soul be strengthened, ambition inspired, and success achieved."

> Seasons of suffering are often the journey to anything worth achieving, the necessary catalysts for helping separate us from self-interests that oppose the greater good.

These amazing women remind us that seasons of suffering are often the journey to anything worth achieving, the necessary catalysts for helping separate us from self-interests that oppose the greater good. These seasons also help us develop deeper compassion. We are no longer quick to offer a simple formula to fix someone's heartache, having recognized in our own lives how ineffective those strategies can be in the face of great disappointment or anguish.

When I finally learned to look past the lack of recognition and instead channel my energies toward creating my own opportunities, my need for recognition seemed to fade. I still appreciate recognition, but the need for it has taken a backseat to the need to constantly expand my horizons and to create for myself the opportunities that I desire most.

For example, I had been working at Deloitte in Tulsa for about a year and a half and longed to be transferred to New York City. My boss was busy with his own projects and didn't seem to recognize my sense of urgency to make it happen.

I was concurrently working on a national project team I'd volunteered for at the firm in an attempt to create opportunities for networking and experience. As a result of my work on that project, I had been recognized by a partner with whom I connected on a personal and professional level. She invited me to attend one of her meetings in Washington, D.C.

A national marketing director for the firm happened to also be attending. I did not know at the time, but he had heard of my interest in a transfer and invited me to dinner the night before the meeting. I had no idea that over Spanish tapas, he was scouting out my interest to see whether an opening he had in New York might be a fit.

I remember calling my mom the day the D.C. meeting finished, feeling more discouraged about the potential of a transfer than I had felt in a long, long time. Meanwhile, the national marketing director was leaving the same meeting, putting in motion a way to get me to NYC to fill his open position.

Within the next four weeks, I flew to New York, interviewed with the partners I'd be working for, negotiated a deal with the firm for the new salary and moving package, and began working with a broker to find an apartment in Manhattan. Three months after the D.C. meeting, I was living in New York, starting a new job.

> The more you can channel your energy toward scouting the horizon for new perspectives, new people, and new challenges in your current work, the more you will find a growing satisfaction and excitement emerge in your heart.

This experience is proof to me that we never really understand all that is being orchestrated in our lives. Right now, you have no idea what all is in motion for you. So don't quit now!

Letting go of the need for recognition is tough, but the more you can channel your energy toward scouting the horizon for new perspectives, new people, and new challenges in your current work, the more you will find a growing satisfaction and excitement emerge in your heart. In the meantime, as you begin to expand your view, here are a few simple ways to satisfy the reasonable need for recognition:

*Depend on the right friends.* Surround yourself with friends and colleagues who recognize your value and are a regular encouragement to you.

*Get involved.* Choose extracurricular activities (personal or professional) that utilize the broad spectrum of your talents.

*Keep a running list.* Maintain a list of your achievements for your own review. Even small things are worth recording. When you get discouraged, read through this list and remind yourself of the difference you are making even when few others seem to notice. I had a "drawer of encouragement" in my desk at the university that was full of thank-you notes and cards sent by alumni and friends. These were a great encouragement when I was frustrated or downcast.

*Be grateful.* When your boss or others express recognition, be grateful and enjoy those moments, even if they occur less often than you would hope for. I recently received a gift certificate as a thank-you for an innovative new program I developed and deployed. I felt as though it should've been ten times more than what I received, but instead of bemoaning the size of the gift, I received it with gratitude and splurged on a very fun leopard-and-lavender Coach purse, one I never would have bought on my own. Now when I use this bag, I remember the recognition and it makes me smile.

*Be excellent.* Don't forget the most important thing you must do, regardless of how you feel right now. No matter what, you must be excellent, doing the job as if you had the biggest title, the best office, and the most substantial paycheck. Take on what author Todd Duncan calls a "CEO mindset." Whether or not you're the CEO in title, you are the CEO of your career.[7] Barbara Walters put it cleverly when she told TV host Joan Lunden early in her career, "Take every crumb they throw you and handle them magnificently."[8]

## WHEN YOU FEEL UNDERPAID

I have come to realize that almost everyone, at some point, perhaps at many points, struggles with feeling underpaid. There are times when I knew I was grossly underpaid in contrast to the market, yet I chose to remain in that job for reasons beyond compensation.

Choice is one of the most freeing ways to deal with seasons when you believe you are underpaid. Remember that in the end you really do have a choice. You can look for another job, add another job, work within your current job to move to a higher position, or negotiate a pay raise.

Of course, I don't know all your specific roadblocks and hindrances, but if you think outside your own box for a minute, you will probably discover ways that you can increase your pay or make what you do now bring value beyond money while working toward something more.

As with the issues of being unrecognized and underutilized, the key when feeling underpaid is creating your own opportunities versus thinking that those above you or beyond you are in control of your finances.

Anyone who has worked for a nonprofit can tell you that such a career is not typically about getting rich. Rather, it's about building a vision that is bigger than the paycheck. I learned this lesson best during the ten years I worked for my alma mater. I began to remind myself that I really did have choices. I started to feel more content with my paycheck while working on strategies that would ultimately lead to more income.

> The key when feeling underpaid is creating your own opportunities versus thinking that those above you or beyond you are in control of your finances.

While earning less than you want or deserve, you can be building on skills, connections, and opportunities that can ultimately lead to greater earning power. While I was at the university, I began to create my own tools and templates to use with my small staff. These are now part of the leadership programs I teach around the country.

As you are working, here are a few practical ways to deal with the seasons in your life when you may feel you are underpaid:

*Be informed.* Research the job market (via the Internet or industry publications) to understand what the market is paying for your job and for someone with your education or experience. This helps you be realistic about your current situation.

*Talk to others.* Find people in comparable positions or at similar companies in order to determine whether your financial situation is as dire as it seems to you.

*Recognize you have choices.* Think about all the choices you have to generate the income you need or desire. Are there ways you can add to your current income outside of getting a raise? Can you create these additions in ways that complement your current work instead of just providing more money? The more connected your entire work life is, the more valuable and synergized your skills and networks become.

*Consider what you are gaining.* Focus on the ways you are building your personal value, such as growing your skills, adding to your résumé, broadening your networks, and educating yourself on the industry in which you serve. Remind yourself that these are valuable, essential aspects of your long-term earning power.

*Be content for now.* Once you have done your research, analyzed your options, and begun to broaden your perspective, choose to be content and accept the place you're in as an education and unique opportunity. If you've determined to remain in your current circumstances for a little longer, then make the most of them. This acceptance will do wonders for your attitude and feelings of empowerment.

*Stay positive.* Be grateful that you are earning a living, and focus on the positives that you are gaining in this season. I often run through a list of all that I'm grateful for in my job, even little things like being able to dress up and look professional, or the interesting people I meet, or the training I'm receiving on my company's dime. The list typically goes on much further than I might think and helps me stay positive and grateful for what I am receiving beyond compensation.

## WHAT LEADERS MUST DO
In chapter 7, I focus more broadly on leadership tools and strategies; but it is fitting at this point to address a few simple things leaders can do in the areas of recognizing, utilizing, and compensating employees. My own personal disappointments through the years have prompted my dedication to address these issues consistently with those I lead.

I make it a point to know and understand each person on my team, committing to their personal purpose and passion to the point of taking them through annual team-building days and weekly one-on-ones in which we focus on their interests and dreams. It is astounding how much motivation, trust, and loyalty is built between people both up the chain and across the team when you acknowledge what's in their hearts, help them craft a plan that aligns their current work with their broader purpose, and encourage them to make strides toward their dreams.

## No One Appreciates Me Around Here!

One company who gets this is McKinney, a leading creative agency based in Durham, North Carolina, whose client roster includes Audi of America, Travelocity, and the NASDAQ Stock Market. The CEO asks each employee to write out his or her dream job performance for the coming year. He then expects each leader to help craft an environment where this performance can be achieved. McKinney, which last year interviewed 4,580 people (in person) to fill 134 vacancies, understands just how critical it is to create career paths that become the jobs where the best people choose to be.

If you can't pay someone more or enough, you can at least give what doesn't cost an out-of-pocket dime—the affirmation, recognition, and brainstorming of options to fully utilize their breadth of skills. This costs so little yet pays huge dividends in the end, including the undeniable satisfaction and joy in being a leader who invests in others, growing people toward greatness time and again.

Here are a few quick tips to make this difference on a regular basis:

*List who is on your team and record what they have done lately.* Make a list of your direct reports (if it's a huge number, start with just a few). List three things you appreciate about each person and something specific you can do to communicate each one of these (i.e., leave a voice mail, drop an e-mail, write a personal note, stop them in the hall to tell them, share it at a staff meeting). Do whatever seems best to you, but don't be afraid to step outside your comfort zone as well.

*Decide how can you recognize them.* What have they recently accomplished that would be worthy of recognition or some kind of reward? Write down what you will do to recognize and/or reward them. Be creative.

*Review their compensation.* Should they be paid more? Complete a salary survey for comparable jobs. If you can, work toward better alignment with market scales, or at a minimum let them know you're informed and will do your best to make progress.

*Keep meeting like this.* Set up regular one-on-one meetings in which you talk about more than work. Ask questions and listen; watch what makes their eyes light up. This will be a good method for understanding what's really in their hearts. Even if you're unable to make a sizable difference now, the fact that you asked and listened will deepen their trust and respect in powerful ways.

There are no silver bullets in leadership, and it is up to every individual you lead to ultimately find his or her own place of satisfaction and reward. At the same time, leaders should always seek to answer a few crucial questions each of us is asking.

Licensed therapist Mary Bellofatto suggests that these three are being asked regardless of a person's position or title:

1. *Can anyone see me?* Don't see me for what I have or my titles; look beyond the externals and see my soul and spirit.
2. *Can anyone hear me?* In a world that doesn't listen anymore, I need to be heard.
3. *Can anyone approve of me?* Tell me I am acceptable and recognize me for my efforts.[9]

> **Making a point to appreciate, recognize, and reward those around us is part of what makes leadership so fulfilling.**

Whether we do it for ourselves or for those we are leading, making a point to appreciate, recognize, and reward those around us is part of what makes leadership so fulfilling. At first it can feel like one more thing on a list of things that rarely get done. However, when we prioritize these acts of serving those we lead, the dividends show up quickly in results such as greater commitment, less resistance, lower turnover, and better morale. These improvements in turn make our jobs as leaders more rewarding.

The French philosopher Voltaire understood this truth in the eighteenth century when he said, "Appreciation is a wonderful thing; it makes what is excellent in others belong to us as well."

*I know what it feels like to be that broke and to live through it and not to know it's about to change. That's the crucial thing. I couldn't see any light at the end of the tunnel.*

—J. K. ROWLING
Author of the Harry Potter book series

# FOUR

# Is This All I'm Working For?
# There Must Be Something More!

**S**tanding in the airport bookstore like I do twice each week, scanning the beautiful covers of the latest home décor and fashion magazines, a slight pang of guilt hits. I think, *I should be using the time to read the* Wall Street Journal *or the latest issue of* Fortune *instead.* So I drag my carry-on bag to the business section.

One or two covers look interesting, but soon I am drawn back to the allure of *Elle Décor* and *Harper's Bazaar.* What would be the most fun to read on this trip? Something on fashion? Food? Decorating? They all appeal to me more than the stock trends and corporate how-tos sitting there on the left. Eventually, to avoid the guilt from either decision, I buy one of each and head to my gate.

The dilemma at the magazine wall illustrates a challenge I've confronted for the past twenty years. It's one that many women I talk to also face: wishing that our work lives were as alluring to the whole of our minds and hearts as our personal hobbies and dreams seem to be.

I hear of women who love their work so much that they're up until all hours of the morning writing e-mails and reading articles about their chosen profession. But that has not been me much of the time. Instead, I'm on the phone after work with girlfriends like Leslie, never married and forty-five, who tells me on her walk up Fifth Avenue to her chic apartment, "People think I'm so savvy and into my work because I work for Donald Trump, but honestly, I'd trade all of this for the joy of supporting a husband and carpooling kids instead."

Maybe we don't all want the *Leave It to Beaver* life, but we all seem to yearn for something more than work can give us. A recent article in the *New York Times* seems to support this notion. Women in elite colleges across the nation, when asked about their career aspirations, indicated an overwhelming preference for marriage and children, if not immediately, at least in the future, and an unwillingness to sacrifice these dreams for their careers.[1]

Not all of us are waiting for marriage or children, but maybe we share a common feeling—a nagging question—one we hesitate to admit or address.

*Is this all there really is?*

While this question lies on one end of the spectrum, there is another one that seems similarly connected to our desire for long-term fulfillment.

*How long must I wait?*

I recently addressed a crowd of five hundred women in New York City, women from all over the nation who were attending this opening session of a conference.

> We share a
> common feeling—a
> nagging question—
> one we hesitate to
> admit or address.
> *Is this all there
> really is?*

"Everyone in this room is waiting for something," I began. Then I listed a few things women are often waiting for, such as the following:

- the relationship of our dreams;
- our body to be healthy again;
- financial provision;
- a crucial resolution or direction during a time of testing;
- pregnancy and a child;

- a wayward child to come home;
- a marriage to be restored.

Heads all over the audience nodded in agreement, thinking about the one or more desires they had yet to realize.

## THE CHALLENGE: I STILL LONG FOR MORE

While most of us seem to possess much, it seems that we are still often waiting for something more.

Waiting is not one of my better skills, I must admit. I am naturally impatient and consider waiting a real waste most of the time. I approach checkout lines by analyzing which one will be the fastest, then end up frustrated when I hear, "Price check on aisle nine."

I mentioned in the previous chapter how painful it was to wait those eight years for the promised promotion, salary increase, and recognition. I often complained during that season, convinced that the seemingly endless wait was a grand waste of my precious time.

My attitude may have been advanced by living in our American society. Waiting is generally not encouraged or rewarded. Consider the following:

- Wait more than thirty minutes for your pizza, and you deserve to have it for free.
- Don't wait until you have the cash; buy now and pay no interest for six months.
- Want your photos fast? We can have them ready in an hour.
- Want your online purchase faster? Pay a premium fee and you'll have it tomorrow.
- Want those pounds off quicker? Take these pills and see results in thirty days.

BlackBerries, search engines, and cell phones have taught us that what we want is just a few keystrokes away. We are used to self-directed inquiries and instant responses.

Sadly, this subtle yet ongoing message does not serve us well and can lead to

63

an overriding sense of constant discontent. We become dissatisfied with what we have and would rather not wait to make things better. We want life to be better, more fulfilling, more suited for us right now.

Truth is, some things are better when we wait.

Imagine deciding to have a baby, and just a week after conception your baby is born. No nine months to get prepared. No time for baby showers and shopping, not to mention what a shock it would be to your body. What painful stretch marks!

> **Truth is, some things are better when we wait.**

Far too many of us know the pain that results from not waiting until we can actually afford something. Credit cards, while a handy convenience, are creating financial pressures at an all-time high. The Consumer Credit Counseling Service estimates that 20 percent of Americans have maxed out their credit cards, and today's average credit card debt is $8,400 per household.[2]

Waiting is often a crucial time of preparation and refocusing. It is a chance to assess our progress thus far and contemplate what still lies ahead.

## UNFULFILLED DESIRES

In an interview with Katie Couric a few years ago, J. K. Rowling, author of the Harry Potter books, spoke of the days before her dreams transpired. She'd been a single mom living on welfare who would write from a local café while her daughter slept in the stroller. At the time of her interview with Couric, five years and five books later, she was remarried, she had a new baby boy, and her fortune was worth an estimated $500 million. "I know what it feels like to be that broke," she explained, "and to live through it and not to know it's about to change. That's the crucial thing. I couldn't see any light at the end of the tunnel."[3]

At no time in my own life has the light been dimmer than during my long, unplanned, unwanted wait for marriage and family.

Many women I know talk of this particular desire as one that seems to tarry longer than most of us ever wish or believe it will. A recent survey of 36,000 single men and women found that more than 84 percent who are thirty-one years of age or older are ready to commit to a new relationship, while 61 percent below the age of thirty-one are ready.[4] And then there are those—some 52 percent—whose marriages don't last.[5] For many, this leaves them more discouraged than when they were single.

As long as I can remember, more than anything I wanted to get married and have a family. As a young girl, I expressed these dreams through the "Barbie universe" my sister and I created in our basement. My Barbie doll had blonde hair like mine, and Brenda's had brown hair like hers. Our Ken dolls were identical, so our story of their lives was that identical twin brothers married fraternal twin sisters, and each couple had one daughter: Skipper for me, and Skipper's friend for Brenda. We played for hours on end and through their lives envisioned our own joyful futures.

I did not date much in high school. I wanted to but was never really pursued. I didn't go to any of my high school proms but did attend one at another school with a family friend. Our prom picture sadly captured my lot with men at the time—the two of us slightly smiling, his arms awkwardly posed around mine, and his eyes completely closed!

How well that picture portrayed my teenage years. Every guy I was interested in just didn't see me. My mom, always the encourager and woman of great faith, told me it was because God was protecting me from bad situations by putting a veil over their eyes so that I would not be misused or make regrettable mistakes. My mind wanted to believe her words, but my heart kept longing to be in love.

Many women I know express similar longings and endure lengthy, difficult seasons of waiting for marriage or for other dreams. My friend Cheryl Cutlip, a Radio City Rockette and assistant choreographer for the Radio City Christmas Spectacular, never expected her season of suffering to be what it was. She and I were catching up over lunch recently, reflecting on this part of her story.

I had been a Rockette for twelve years and was on a growth track professionally. During that time I got married and after a few years was joyfully pregnant. At six months, our son Stuart was born prematurely because of a physical condition I did not know I had. Three days later he died.

I had to physically deal with the trauma, having an emergency C-section, wondering if I'd really be able to dance again. It was so difficult to look physically like I had had a baby but have no baby in my arms. Then also I was dealing with it on a spiritual level. We had been praying for that baby every day, so reconciling the loss emotionally and spiritually in my heart was a process.

As a performer, it's about being joyful and giving the gift of dance from your heart. It took time to recover, and the long season of being out of sync professionally was a challenge.[6]

Cheryl's story of suffering is one I relate to very well. Waiting into my early forties for my dream of marriage and family to transpire, I would often wrestle between hope and despair, questioning how the wait could in any way be preparation. I was challenged to celebrate the joy of virtually all my friends receiving the dreams of *my* heart. I watched my sister marry and have a baby. I was increasingly lonely, with viable husband options decreasing with each passing year.

My wait, and that of so many others around me, prompted me to look for answers about the seemingly universal dilemma of perpetually wanting something we still don't have.

In my conversation with Merrill Lynch executive Westina Matthews Shatteen, she explained what she learned during times of great hopelessness and despair. It's a great lesson for each of us.

I know what it is to be in a loveless marriage, to have no money, not to know how you'll pay the rent or put food on the table. I've worn socks on my hands as gloves in Chicago when it was so cold. In remembering these times, though, I also remember that I did get through them. "Yea though I walk *through* the valley of the shadow of death," as it says in Psalm 23. Every day I get up and thank God for the day. I'm confident that I'm one day closer to the resolution, to where I'm meant to be.[7]

## THE CYCLE OF DISCONTENTMENT

I'll never forget one lunch hour when this struggle for contentment and resolution played out in front of my eyes. I was hurrying into the mall, dressed in a suit, pantyhose, and some favorite high heels. As I approached the door, a cute, casually dressed young mother pushing her towheaded two-year-old son in a stroller was approaching the same entrance.

*She has the life I want,* I thought. *How much fun it must be to not wear painful shoes and pantyhose in the summertime, no pressure to be back to work in just an*

66

*hour, enjoying the fulfillment of raising your little one.*

Just then, the young mother made a comment that jarred me out of my envious daydream. "Oh, you look so nice!" she said warmly. "How fun to dress up for work and have a real job."

I wanted to grab her hand and let her know just what I had been thinking. *I want your life and you want mine!* The truth was, we both had something great, but looking over the fence into the yard next door, we both saw more green.

Some years later, the scenario repeated itself as my friend Jennifer and I were riding around in her van one Saturday afternoon. We had just finished touring the beautifully decorated home she shared with her husband, Mark, and their five children. She said, "Lynette, you have the life I always envisioned having. I dreamed of having a career and working for many years, maybe living in a big city, pursuing my dreams. Instead, I met Mark early and dove full-time into his work and our kids."

At this point I confessed, "And I always envisioned your life, Jennifer. Here I am still waiting for a husband and kids." She and I laughed. Then I asked her, "Do you want to know my take on all this?" She nodded. I then shared with her the conclusion I reached after the mall incident.

One of the most common temptations women face is lack of contentment. In fact, if you know the story of Adam and Eve, it was this exact temptation that the serpent used with Eve. In the garden of perfection, in perfect harmony with her husband and every creature of the land, she wanted the one thing she didn't have.

Women are by nature "fixers," so we focus incessantly on fixing our wait. We believe the lie that if we had that one thing

> Women are by nature "fixers," so we focus incessantly on fixing our wait. We believe the lie that if we had that one thing for which we are waiting, everything in our world would be better.

for which we are waiting, everything in our world would be better. But because there is always something more we could want, the cycle of discontentment is unending:

- We're single and want a husband.
- We're married and want a child.
- We have kids and then can't wait until they're in school so we can get our time back.
- We are at home with our children and miss our outside work.
- We stay at work and feel guilty that we are not home with our children.
- Working, we wish for more time off and the freedom to pursue our bigger dreams.
- The bigger dreams come, and we long for the good old days of leisure.

Lasting contentment is elusive for every woman I know. If you find a woman who is content with her life, listen to her story. I'll bet she has discovered a few of the following strategies that I discovered once I realized discontentment had become a lingering, unwanted companion.

## THE STRATEGY: DISCOVER GIFTS
## IN SURPRISING PLACES

If you find yourself wondering if this is all there is, longing for something more, you are certainly not alone. Hundreds of women I've worked with through the years, many extremely successful in their careers, speak to me of their "other dreams." By that, they mean their deepest desires that remain unfulfilled.

If I have learned one key to maintaining joy amid waiting, it is this: somewhere in each of our lives, clouded at times by a lack of understanding and perspective, are gifts waiting to be celebrated. Often they're right in front of us.

- Leo Gerstenzang thought of Q-tips when he saw his wife trying to clean their baby's ears with toothpicks and cotton.
- Ott Diffenbach came up with soda straws when he twisted the wrapper from a cigarette pack and saw he had created a tube.
- Charles Strite was fuming at the burned toast in the factory lunchroom when he thought up the toaster.[8]
- Spencer Silver discovered the temporary Post-It Note adhesive while searching for one that was permanent and strong.[9]

Sometimes in surprising places, gifts appear. We would receive many more, I believe, if we were actively looking for them.

Our struggles and yearnings, if viewed as a pathway of preparation instead of a vehicle for bitterness, will work a hope, patience, and inspiration into our lives not likely to emerge without the struggle. Holocaust survivor Viktor Frankl said it best when he wrote, "What is to give light must endure burning."

> Our struggles and yearnings, if viewed as a pathway of preparation instead of a vehicle for bitterness, will work a hope, patience, and inspiration into our lives not likely to emerge without the struggle.

When we celebrate what we have now, our hearts grow in their capacity to feel and experience more of life with all its varied challenges, and to discover hope when possibilities seem far away.

Celebrating the process means that we shift our focus off our yet unfulfilled dreams to the reasons all around us we have to be grateful. Sometimes in my darkest hours, I would make a list of reasons to be joyful. Things like living in a free country, the ability to be educated, parents who have stayed married for forty-nine years, physical and emotional health, deep and meaningful friendships, my faith, great books to read, and the ability to read itself. And there's so much more. Practicing gratefulness is a simple exercise, yet it's a powerful weapon against the enemies of discouragement, self-pity, and hopelessness that we all succumb to at times.

Celebrating the process also means that we choose to enjoy the unique benefits of the season we're in now, both at work and in our personal lives. As a single woman, I had the freedom to spend and invest my money however I wanted. I could take a spontaneous vacation with a girlfriend, eat at New York's finest restaurants, frequently attend Broadway shows, and schedule anything without the permission of anyone. I didn't have to cook for a family, and sometimes I had to stop and think about the simple joy of pouring a bowl of Cheerios for dinner, throwing a baked potato in the microwave, or ordering out with no one complaining about the choice.

These kinds of reminders are essential during times of frustration, discouragement, or impatience over unfulfilled desires and dreams. The battle to stay joyful is primarily a battle of the mind. I have recognized that there are certain ways of thinking that I must continually choose and others I need to avoid. I call it the ongoing battle between life-giving and life-taking choices. It is something that applies in so many areas of life.

Under these two headings, consider your thoughts, the people you know, the foods you eat, the words you speak. Are they life-giving or life-taking? Here are some examples:

| Life-Giving | Life-Taking |
|---|---|
| Fostering relationships | Choosing to be isolated |
| Remaining active | Being lazy |
| Eating healthy foods | Eating junk food |
| Being positive | Complaining |
| Encouraging others | Gossiping |

It is especially crucial during the strenuous times of waiting that we make life-giving choices. The way I finally lost the twenty pounds I gained in college was not by dieting but by adding life-giving foods to my diet, which in turn caused me to hunger less for the things that retained extra weight.

Instead of eliminating all fatty or high-carb foods, I committed to eating at least "five alive" foods each day. That meant adding "alive" foods to my diet, things like raw nuts, yogurt, fruits and vegetables, and seeds. As I focused on eating at least five alive foods daily, slowly I began to lose weight. Eventually, I retrained my palate to prefer life-giving foods, a pattern I maintain today.

Most of us tend toward life-taking choices. Something about our human nature seems to point us away from the things that are best. As purpose-motivated people of greatness and the only real stewards of our lives, we cannot just casually happen upon outcomes. We must take a good, hard look at our choices, understand how they are impacting results, and then make new life-giving choices instead.

When I find it hard to give up certain things, I focus on adding something life-giving. Rather than getting rid of my cheese Danish for breakfast, I'll add a banana or small bowl of high-fiber cereal, which I eat first. The fullness I receive from the life-giving foods helps me say no to the Danish most of the time.

The many times I attended wedding showers and baby showers while single, I had to guard my mind from feeling left out or sorry for myself. This wasn't always easy and required a discipline of the mind. Instead of launching a mental pity party, I would choose to look at the blessing of my friends as a sign of hope for my own life and trust that what happened for them could happen for me as well.

The more often I made this choice, the more natural the thinking became, so instead of the many years of showers causing increasing bitterness, they actually became easier to enjoy. I could attend the parties and even throw the showers, investing in the joy of others without being launched into days of despair and pain.

When your sense of feeling left out, passed over, and forgotten rears its ugly head, simply choose to believe that there is a bigger plan at work. At the end of the day, it really is a choice—a choice to believe instead of not believe, a choice to hope instead of becoming hopeless, a choice to wait when waiting seems to be more than you can endure.

In those times (and they have been many), I have made the decision to choose to believe. I do this because at the end of my life, I would rather be a woman who was hopeful, even if my dreams remain unfulfilled, than be a woman who was complacent, not caring one way or another because believing is just too messy and scary. My confidence lies in a bigger, greater, more powerful plan at work, one that will turn out great in the end. And so I choose to believe.

The more I have practiced this pattern of productive thinking, the easier it has become to stay in that mode and, as a result, maintain joy most of the time.

One woman I know who seems to have done this with great success is Denise Johnston, formerly president and chief merchandising officer at Liz Claiborne and now president of the adult division at The Gap. Denise, who is single and lives in New York, lives one of the most fulfilling lives of anyone I know. In a recent conversation, she captured what I took to be a few of her keys to success in building a rich, satisfying life.

One of the things I have loved about every one of my jobs is the people, beginning in college and in every job since. When I come across difficult times or joyful times,

71

it's the love of family and friends that matters most. As much as I may love my job, it's not the main love. What the jobs have brought is the love of friendships over the years.

I work really, really hard on this part of my life. I make time to go visit my girlfriend in Italy a couple of times a year, or my best friend from Minneapolis. We go skiing or she comes out to my house on Long Island. My friend from California and I go to the south of France, or I go to her house and spend long weekends with her and her family. I tie in my love of travel and the fact I do it for work as a way to be with my friends, making the most of any free time to bring life back into my spirit.[10]

## HOW TO CELEBRATE DURING A SEASON OF WAITING

Here are some of my favorite, practical ways I celebrate while waiting. Try them for yourself.

*Record why you're grateful.* Jot down in a journal all the things you have to be grateful for right now. Write them out in detail; meditate on *why* they are worth celebrating. If you have a hard time coming up with these, ask a friend or family member to list some for you. Then be thankful for every last one of them. And tomorrow, be thankful again!

*Remember your dreams.* The British poet Emily Dickinson once confessed, "Not knowing when the dawn will come, I open every door." Spend time regularly describing the things you are still waiting for and imagine the possibilities. At the same time, look for threads of hope in the things you already have. Open the doors of your mind and heart as you think about what still awaits you.

*Acknowledge the perks.* Consider what unique advantages accompany the season of life you're in now. What experiences are you having that other seasons will not afford you? What are you learning from these unique experiences that you can take with you into the next season? How can you celebrate the perks of this season? Be creative, and if you find it difficult to do so, ask someone else to think with you.

Traveling for work was something I had to do a lot as a single woman. Occasionally, I would ask my mom to join me, or I would stay over on a weekend and explore fun places with friends who lived there. Now that I'm married, it's not as easy or convenient to travel for work, and how grateful I am that I took advantage during those single years to see the world and to foster so many valuable friendships.

*Listen to those who know.* What books have been written about the experiences of your life right now? Find authors whose biographies read like yours and gain insights from their stories. Think about how you might write your own story. Even jot down ideas on the lessons your story would produce for others. What would you want them to leave with after reading it? As you do this, keep in mind what activist Marian Wright Edelman, founder of the Children's Defense Fund, says: "We must not, in trying to think about how we can make a big difference, ignore the small daily differences we can make which, over time, add up to big differences that we often cannot foresee." Make a difference in your life now; write chapters worth reading, even as you wait for the grander story to unfold.

> **Why not create our own personal benefits work plans to ensure that our lives right now live up to their fullest potential?**

*Log your life lessons.* Organize a file entitled "Lessons from My Life Thus Far." Regularly fill it with the lessons you learn or are learning in this season. As my speaking career began growing, I was constantly amazed at how my stories of struggle and frustration, accompanied by the hope I chose to have in spite of them, encouraged my audiences time and again. As I saw my journey spur others on to hope and not compromise, I began searching more diligently for new insights and lessons in each mountain and valley.

My Rockette friend, Cheryl, and her husband, Ron, went on to have a precious daughter, Ava. Cheryl told me how amazed she is that her story of suffering and finding faith to make it through has helped many people find hope themselves.[11] By seeing our individual journeys as lights for others who follow, we can more easily recognize the lessons and gifts we are receiving.

## YOUR PERSONAL BENEFITS WORK PLAN

In addition to salary, personal benefits comprise a significant part of most compensation packages. *Fortune's* "Most Admired Companies" are often noted for their innovative approach to employee benefits.[12] On-site child care, free health-club memberships, personal life coaches, flexible work arrangements—these are just a few of the most common benefits many of us are enjoying these days.

But the truth is that we don't have to rely on our employers to offer such things. Why not create our own personal benefits work plans to ensure that our lives right now live up to their fullest potential? Here's one way to do this.

Using something similar to the chart below, begin by writing your purpose statement at the top. Then, in the categories listed in the chart (or add your own), outline the benefits you can enjoy or create out of what you already have. This chart works for any season of life. Take a look at the examples below, and then create your own chart to coincide with the season you're in now. This is usually an eye-opening exercise.

My Purpose Statement: _____

| Season I'm in Now | Perks That Go with It | How to Maximize the Perks |
|---|---|---|
| Singleness | Freedom to travel<br><br>Can eat out and just pay for one person<br><br>Can set own schedule | Stay over on weekends.<br><br>Meet a friend in the city.<br><br>Set up time to go to Jean George's new restaurant.<br><br>Check into NYC Ballet tickets. |
| Working a ton of hours | Building my résumé<br><br>Training on the company's dime<br><br>Meeting interesting people at work | Keep record of and describe personal contributions, add to résumé.<br><br>Update my Rolodex; consider what clients I'm meeting on assignments; focus on pulling them into my business network (i.e., relationships I can call on in the future). |

| Season I'm in Now | Perks That Go with It | How to Maximize the Perks |
|---|---|---|
| Empty nest | Time to take golf lessons<br>No need to cook as much<br>Freedom to travel | Get involved in community service outlets.<br>Do pro bono work using my career credentials for causes I'm passionate about.<br>Do consulting on special projects that are of interest.<br>Become more active as a board member; lead a committee.<br>Teach classes at the local university<br>Train for the NYC Marathon. |
| Between jobs | Time to explore new career options<br>Chance to get back in touch with old contacts | Update my résumé.<br>Reignite my exercise routine.<br>Read *What Color Is Your Parachute?* and consider new options. |

## WHAT ARE YOU WAITING FOR?

As I closed my talk with the five hundred women at the NYC conference that weekend, I asked them, "*What* are you waiting for?" Then I asked it again, with a different emphasis: "What are you *waiting* for?"

That is the question I am posing to you as well. Begin living now. Not when your wait is over and your current dreams transpire. Not when circumstances improve and

Now is the time. Don't miss even one perk that this season affords; there are more than you think.

75

changes come. Now is the time. Don't miss even one perk that this season affords; there are more than you think. Be the kind of person who looks back on every season with gratefulness and looks ahead for the gifts yet to come.

Former British prime minister Margaret Thatcher captured this spirit well. "Look at a day," she explained, "when you are supremely satisfied at the end. It's not a day when you lounge around doing nothing; it's when you had everything to do, and you've done it."

As the only woman ever to serve as prime minister in the United Kingdom, and as the longest-serving British prime minister in the twentieth century, Mrs. Thatcher knows something about what it takes to succeed. If she had waited for permission or to find a role model, she might very well still be waiting.

Gutsy women like her inspire us to move assertively forward while never losing sight of all the gifts we are receiving along the way. Their lives challenge us to be grateful for every small gift, including those we did not choose or realize we needed. An Estonian proverb I like summarizes this so well: "Who does not thank for little, will not thank for much."

Be thankful now, and you will have much to be thankful for later. What are you waiting for?

*I encourage people who find themselves in a position where their current work is not getting them energized and excited about being there, to first and foremost continue doing a great job. . . . I was working at one point for someone who did not support me, so I found a way out of his group. Three years later I found myself working for him again.*

—JOYCE ROCHE
CEO and President, Girls Inc.

# FIVE

# I'm Unrecognized, Unappreciated, and Underpaid!

Promotion isn't something we think about when we're young. We experience it without doing much more than showing up. If we complete the basics and follow the rules, we get promoted—from kindergarten to grade school, fifth grade to middle school, eighth grade to high school, and then high school to college if we choose.

Once we begin our careers, it is only natural to expect promotions to come in a similar way. Many of us, women in particular, do what we believe is expected, pass the tests, follow the rules, and seem to be moving forward quite well. When a promotion doesn't happen, we're often puzzled or taken aback.

The good news is that moving up the proverbial ladder is not as complicated as it might seem. It doesn't necessarily require working for the perfect company or the ideal boss, bragging about yourself, or stepping on people's toes to get to the next rung. It does, however, require more than we were used to giving in school.

Promotion requires a possibility-laden outlook and some creative energy directed in a few strategic, proactive ways. Here's what I mean.

## THE CHALLENGE: I NEED TO CREATE BIGGER AND BETTER OPPORTUNITIES

We included in the subheading of this book "Ten Strategies for Stepping Up to Success and Satisfaction." The question is, how do we actually step up? Do we do the stepping, or does someone have to pull us up? Let me offer a couple of illustrations that demonstrate two ways of approaching career promotion.

The first shows the typical "satisfaction cycle" most people experience as they move from job to job throughout their careers.

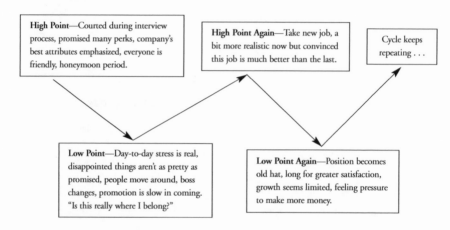

This second diagram is a more ideal picture of how our career should be.

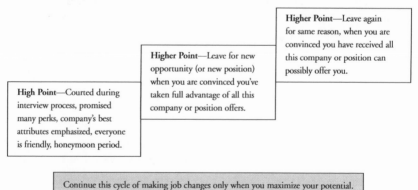

### I'm Unrecognized, Unappreciated, and Underpaid!

Most people move up and down in a never-ending roller coaster of high expectations and deep disappointment. Each honeymoon period ends, and we find ourselves caught in the daily grind, working hard and wondering if there isn't something better out there.

The average worker will have twelve job changes over her working lifetime, and these transitions often occur at low points of frustration over a disappointing or less-than-expected job.[1] For a time, our spirits then lift as we are relieved to be rid of the people and problems of an old job and free to dive into something new. Unfortunately, in a matter of time, the new job feels surprisingly familiar except for a few different faces and names. We're on a descent again.

> **We have to remember that success and significance are not meant for later—they can be achieved by using everything we currently have at our disposal.**

Let's say for a minute that we do something else instead. Let's climb into the driver's seats of our careers and realize that we have many choices at many junctures. We make a choice to stay in each position or company until we have fully leveraged it for all it can possibly afford us.

Leveraging the company means maximizing everything we have now, not daydreaming about a fantasy role that hasn't yet come our way. Although it is normal to have an eye on the future and a dream of what is still possible, we have to remember that success and significance are not meant for later—they can be achieved by using everything we currently have at our disposal.

You may find that what you're looking for is right in front of you. You might also find positive characteristics of your job that you hadn't previously considered. In the least, you will find new possibilities for promotion—ones your own leaders might not be seeing for you—right where you stand.

#### INSIDE OPPORTUNITIES

One of my most rewarding career experiences illustrates this point. I had been working at Deloitte for about six years, and many of the things I was teaching in seminars triggered an idea about a program I wanted to design for use at the firm.

It wasn't in my job description and I didn't have permission, but I was passionate about the idea. I shared it one day with a friend from the human resources group who had dropped by my office to say hello. I was eager for his reaction.

I explained the idea for a program that could significantly build employee satisfaction at the firm. "Employees go through a multiweek workshop in which they write their life purpose statement," I began, "and then create a plan to align their current work with that life purpose. The result is that they live out their life purpose right now, here at the firm, and find significantly higher levels of satisfaction in the process. What do you think?"

"Very intriguing," he said. A few weeks later, I found myself in a meeting with him and his boss, the director for human resources in our region and one of the most professional and creative leaders I had met during my time at Deloitte.

He liked the idea, and over the next several months, four of us worked on designing a pilot program that I named "Leading on Purpose™". We solicited applications from some of the brightest men and women, those at the point in their tenure when turnover was typically high. We received tremendous response and two months later were ready to launch.

> When you take new risks and explore new options, it is crucial to keep your current leaders informed.

There was nothing in my current senior marketing manager job description about designing any such program. I spent personal time in the evenings and on weekends working on the content, realizing I could not afford to compromise my current work while trying to create other opportunities. Yet I was so passionate about the idea, spending the personal time was like birthing a new, exciting dream.

Once the pilot program appeared to be a viable possibility, it was time to talk to my boss about the time investment such a pilot would take and gain his consent. I actually wanted more than consent; I wanted his agreement. His support was crucial for any long-term opportunities that might emerge from this new program.

When you take new risks and explore new options, it is crucial to keep your current leaders informed. Even in large companies, you can't afford to make anyone feel disrespected. An effective way to discuss a new idea with anyone, be it your boss, those who work for you, or your colleagues working beside you, is to articulate how the idea or project aligns with their values or goals. It's a win-win principle with a premise that there is enough to go around for everyone—enough time, money, people, and resources—*if* we're creative and approach the situation with a "let's see how this can work" attitude.

Very few people, unfortunately, come to this attitude naturally. Most of those you talk to will feel protective, reluctant, and even afraid to let go of you, your time, money, or whatever new resources might be required for an out-of-the-box idea. This is why most of us simply accept the status quo. Our job is our job, cutbacks are an annual exercise, and resources are on a first-come, first-served basis; so we just do the job, take the money, and consider another option outside the company if it comes. Yet with a little creativity and a "why not?" attitude, you can instigate positive change—positive for you, positive for them.

This pilot program meant a lot to me personally. I knew it was good for the firm. Now it was time to push (or at least persuade) my boss in the same direction.

Emphasizing shared values is always a great place to start. A widely recognized value of Deloitte is helping their employees grow, develop, be trained, and find long-term success at the firm. So as I explained the pilot to my boss, I highlighted how the program would support this companywide value. It would be, in essence, an internal marketing pilot, one that would stretch my abilities and allow me to grow personally and professionally, while simultaneously helping the attendees add value to their work.

I made sure I outlined how much time the program would require, clarified that I would cover my current responsibilities so that nothing would suffer, and emphasized why this was a win-win situation for everyone.

I had been with the firm about six years at this point, with a record of good performance. What this had done for me is create an account of sorts that I was now able to withdraw from. If I had been only half-performing and somewhat disinterested in my work, meeting the mark but not exceeding any goals, my boss would have had little incentive to support me in this endeavor. Fortunately, in the years prior, I had earned his favor and support. He agreed to the pilot and asked that I keep him apprised of the results, which I was happy to do.

The pilot ran and was considered a real success with rave reviews from the participants and the HR leadership team. It opened up doors for a second pilot, and a condensed version of the workshop became another half-day program that my boss asked me to give for the entire marketing team.

## OUTSIDE OPPORTUNITIES

Designing and launching the program provided a valuable new credential for my speaking and writing aspirations. On Deloitte's time, plus a little time of my own, I received something far more valuable than a paycheck.

I stretched beyond my job description to create a bigger and broader opportunity, meeting new people in different roles who in turn helped create even further opportunities. As a result, my satisfaction with my work climbed up the chart during a time when it could have been dipping to a new low.

Eventually, I decided to take the pilot program and others like it outside of Deloitte's walls. I made the decision to move beyond the firm at my highest point of satisfaction and appreciation for all I had received.

I now use the intellectual capital and proprietary material from my program to work with Deloitte and other organizations as an outside consultant, building my own business on the foundation of past work experiences.

Joyce Roche, who sits on several corporate boards and is CEO and president of Girls Inc., told me about how she, too, has mined new opportunities throughout her career, including nineteen years at Avon.

> I encourage people who find themselves in a position where their current work is not getting them energized and excited about being there, to first and foremost continue doing a great job. You never know when it will come back to you. I was working at one point for someone who did not support me, so I found a way out of his group. Three years later I found myself working for him again. Then, do what you need to do to get yourself out of what you don't like. If you stay too long, you get disillusioned and it negatively impacts your work. That really ends up hurting you—not the company or the position, but you. Do what you need to do in your current role, but aggressively look outside that role for other opportunities.[2]

Why not use this same self-empowered concept and begin seeing promotion as something that's in your own hands? This will invigorate you with a sense of power and possibility.

## THE STRATEGY: FOLLOW THE FOUR PRINCIPLES OF PROMOTION AND BUILD YOUR PERSONAL BRAND

As you are preparing for promotion and getting ready to embrace new possibilities, keep in mind what I call the four principles of promotion. These can help you avoid unnecessary delays and better position yourself for every possible promotion, even the opportunities you don't yet see.

### PRINCIPLE #1: PICTURE IT

While your purpose statement defines *why* you are here and doing what you are doing, you will also want many pictures in your mind of where you want to go. Sometimes we call these visions or dreams, both of which help us see how life will look when new successes and satisfaction come our way. I believe it is helpful to have a picture in mind for each major area of your life.

*Personal life.* Picture your relationships with family and friends. Are they life-giving? What kind of investments do you make in them to get the results you need from this most important area of your life? I pictured my husband for many years before he arrived, not so much what he looked like but his character, personality, achievements, the way we were together as a team. This picture helped me wait and move past those who did not seem to fit.

*Professional life.* Picture yourself in the roles that best suit your purpose and abilities. What does it look like when you are there?

I picture certain people at work I want to know, picture myself in leadership roles working in certain divisions, making an impact in certain ways. I was a television major in college and have always wanted to have a television show, so I picture myself sitting on the stage, looking out over the audience, interviewing guests. This picture inspires me to keep moving toward this vision while I wait and hope for it to transpire.

*Spiritual life.* This is an important area for many people. I picture ways I

> While your purpose statement defines *why* you are here and doing what you are doing, you will also want many pictures in your mind of where you want to go.

want to be involved in helping others. I see in my mind the women I want to teach how to live for a cause greater than themselves. I envision how I can continue integrating my personal values into my work.

Corinne McLaughlin, executive director for the Center for Visionary Leadership, knows that women are looking for this connection. She describes this increasingly common desire. "As many more women are entering the workforce," she explains, "they look for companies that are aligned with their spiritual values. Women want to bring their whole selves to work—body, mind, and spirit. They want their spirituality to be more than just faith and belief—they want it to be practical and applied."[3]

*Physical well-being.* I look at pictures in fitness magazines sometimes, and this helps me picture what I want my arms to look like when they're toned, my abs when they're tight, and my legs when I'm maintaining a regular running routine. I peruse healthy recipes and try new things that taste wonderful but don't add weight. This picture is different for everyone and doesn't necessarily have to be dictated by what we see in magazines or other media. These occasionally help me remain motivated to stay healthy and may do the same for you. Other women I know look to role models they know personally. This is an equally inspiring preference.

*Home.* I love to tear out pictures of beautiful rooms, floral arrangements, fabrics, paint swatches, china, and other things that give me a vision for the beauty that I want in my environment. I often browse through these pictures to get a fresh vigor for adding new life to our home.

*Children.* I picture our family many years from now, when the boys are married and have their own children, and how much fun we will have at the holidays. I see them as strong men of character, married to joyful wives with happy children. This picture helps me see beyond the loads of laundry and the carpooling that can sometimes bring stress. It also helps me encourage the boys to be excellent in every way.

The collage of these pictures helps stir my heart and soul over and over again, in good and bad times. The pictures are an encouragement in and of themselves, even when I'm unable to take immediate action on them.

What areas of your life could use a picture of new possibilities? If money and time were not issues, where would you go, what would you do, what would you reach for in the various areas of your life? Consider these things and add to them a picture that will draw you to their culmination.

## PRINCIPLE #2: PLAN FOR IT

Once you have the pictures in your mind, you're ready to create a plan to make them a reality. Pictures remain inanimate without a plan that includes steps to get there.

Ron and I are decorating our home right now, and each room is still in need of many things. Time and money constraints keep us from doing it all at once, but we talk about our plans often. We estimate the costs and determine which months we will invest in new items. This plan helps us continue working toward completing the house. A year from now, the rooms will look more vibrant because we have planned, not just pictured, what can be done.

Your work is like a home awaiting decoration. The foundational structure— your job description, leadership, salary—is set, but there is so much more you can add.

Lisa Sloan-Walker, a business director at Campbell Soup, decorated her career by finding new ways to showcase the company's products. As a junior marketer in the condensed-soup unit, she spotted a fresh advertising tactic. She noticed that many shoppers purchased tomato soup for cooking casseroles and other dishes and proposed promoting the soup as an ingredient instead of as a meal in itself.

"It helped grow the business," she explains. "In the whole scheme of things, it wasn't one of those things that most senior management was focused on, but I created a space for myself and was able to execute it." As a beverages brand manager, she also helped revive the V8 Splash business by linking it with USA swimming. The move gave her great visibility. "I think a lot of women wait to be asked or expect they can work hard and good things will come to them," she says. "I go out there and find people who are willing to listen and help me sell my ideas."[4]

> Your work is like a home awaiting decoration. The foundational structure—your job description, leadership, salary— is set, but there is so much more you can add.

Like Lisa, consider what outside-the-job-description tactics you can execute. Write out the benefits that these efforts will yield for your work both personally and professionally. Then create a plan that will lead you one step closer to promotion, inside the company or outside it.

I've heard my friend Andrea Baumann Lustig explain what she did.

When I had my very first job on Wall Street, I knew I had landed in a fantastic organization. By the end of that job I had developed strong analytical skills and learned a lot about the world of finance. A summer internship led to eleven years in consulting, which was exciting and satisfying. When I made the next move, I knew my skills would transfer well.

**What have you produced recently? Many times we have achieved much but have not taken the time to evaluate or measure our own production.**

Now, instead of helping corporations solve problems, I was focusing on individuals and families. I liked the more individual contact and relationships, but I also had another, more personal objective. I wanted to see if the asset management business was something I could be good at and find interesting. I knew that if I loved it, learned a lot and became successful, I might potentially work in my family's investment management business someday. Turns out it's the very thing I'm doing now, some twenty-five years later.

Looking back, I realize that at each turning point in my career, my plan developed because I consistently asked myself two questions: "What am I good at?" and "What do I enjoy doing?" Then I've looked for opportunities that bring these two elements together.[5]

### PRINCIPLE #3: PRODUCE IT

This is the stage in which you begin to create output and results. You can picture and plan all day long, but production is what will really create the launching pad for promotion.

I tracked the results of the Leading on Purpose program, did extensive evaluations, and put metrics in place so that we could quantify the impact it had on participants. This positioned me for promotion both inside and outside of Deloitte.

What have you produced recently? Many times we have achieved much but have not taken the time to evaluate or measure our own production. If I asked you to describe the last two achievements you have had at work, what would they be? What impact have they had on the company, the people, the bottom line? These are the things you should be regularly recording and, when appropriate, sharing with those who can further your career.

The more picturing and planning you do prior to production, the clearer you will be on the results you achieve.

## PRINCIPLE #4: PATIENTLY WAIT FOR IT

Picturing, planning, and producing will help you be patient without losing hope. Following the first three steps will not guarantee every promotion we want to see. Many times we will simply have to be patient. The good news is that the other three stages keep us occupied with joy and vision while we wait.

Some red stoplights are so long when I'm in a hurry. Unless, that is, I'm putting on lipstick. By the time I dig around in my purse for the lip liner, draw a perfect line, and attempt to fill in with the lipstick, the light has turned green and the impatient guy in the pickup behind me is honking his horn. The same is true when I'm checking my BlackBerry or text-messaging someone. When we're busy and our minds and bodies are engaged, waiting periods don't seem so long.

> One of the best ways to stay busy while anticipating a promotion is to focus on building your personal brand.

Being patient doesn't mean being inactive. Think of the waiter at a busy restaurant. He is a *wait*er, and he's the busiest guy in the place. That's the type of waiter we should be—someone who keeps busy, who stays actively engaged so that those things we're waiting for only occasionally, if at all, bring anxious thoughts or worry.

One of the best ways to stay busy while anticipating a promotion is to focus on building your personal brand. It is something that many women know they need to do but seldom take time to focus on it.

## WHAT IS YOUR PERSONAL BRAND?

Think for a moment about the following women. Using one phrase, how would you describe them?

Oprah Winfrey
Eleanor Roosevelt
Mother Teresa
Martha Stewart

The phrase you chose is, in a nutshell, their reputation. You may not know these women personally, but you can likely describe a bit about them. When you do this, you are telling me about their personal brand.

**Your brand is the sum total of what people think and feel about you.**

Everyone has a personal brand. What is yours? If I ask a few key people in your life about you, what will they say? Your brand is the sum total of what people think and feel about you.

Perhaps those in varying areas of your life would describe you in different ways. While it is true that in our many roles we express varied sides of ourselves, ideally there should be a consistent thread of who we are woven through everything we do.

We describe someone's brand by using adjectives. For example, we might say that Oprah Winfrey is passionate, entrepreneurial, a role model, a trailblazer, an ambassador, articulate. These are all attributes of her personal brand.

How would someone describe you? Is your brand what you want it to be? What are the gaps between how you are perceived in your workplace and how you want to be perceived? These gaps can be proactively managed so that you create the brand you want, live out your purpose, and simultaneously create further opportunities and promotion.

A brand is the promise of the value you'll receive from something or someone. Think about your collection of friends. You know which ones to call when you need motivation, comfort, a good laugh, or a creative idea. Their brand promises you certain results each time you call.

My friend Kim called me one Saturday morning from Paris to get my advice on a shearling coat she found on sale. Was it a good deal? Would she wear it enough to justify the splurge? She called me because she knows my brand promises a trained eye for a great value, something I build on not only personally but also in many aspects of my work.

Think about the e-mails you read and those you don't. The brand of the person sending it determines if it is a priority read or something you file away for later.

Consider the great brands we all know and buy. Names like Nike, Starbucks, McDonald's, Target. These companies go to great lengths and spend millions of dollars each year to build, protect, and grow their brands. When SBC Communications bought AT&T for $16.5 billion, they planned to spend millions on a campaign to relaunch the brand. Some analysts said they could spend hundreds of millions.[6]

My dear friend Lisa Marks, founder and president of her own licensing and marketing agency, gained her expertise developing, building, and marketing brands. She has worked for some of the world's leading entertainment and consumer products companies, such as Disney, Nickelodeon, HBO, and Penguin Publishing. When talking about the essential elements of a strong brand, Lisa highlights qualities like dependability, trust, uniqueness, the ability to consistently satisfy a need or desire, and the delivery of value. She also emphasizes that companies invest a tremendous amount of resources and energy in building their brands, and they do so continuously to foster ongoing development and growth of the business.

She concludes, "If this type of thinking is effective for big companies in building their brands, then why shouldn't we think about making a similar investment and having a strategic focus when building our own personal brand?"[7] I wholeheartedly agree. Only we ourselves care enough to focus on and develop our personal brands.

## MARKETING YOU

In the many "Building Your Personal Brand" workshops I lead, women consistently share the same feedback. They often shy away from building their brands because they are all too familiar with overly aggressive women who brag on themselves and obnoxiously toot their own horns at every turn, just to get ahead. Whether these women draw attention to themselves out of insecurity, unabashed arrogance, or just a plain old lack of tact, it is unattractive and unfeminine to say the least. As a result, many of us decide we won't be like them.

We also have the memory of our mothers telling us, "When you go into a room of people, don't talk about yourself; focus on others." Years later we're escorted into one big room called a workplace, and we realize that if we don't let others know what we've done, no one will. Eventually, we'll be the only

91

one left standing in the room while the rest move on and up to bigger and better things.

A leader at a major firm told me how much he has to coax his female team members to talk about themselves in their year-end self-evaluations. Instead of saying, "I led the engagement team to win $2.5 million in new business," they say, "*We* won $2.5 million in new business." They credit the entire team—which is honorable—but they frequently shy away from mentioning their own notable achievements.

Though I am by nature a marketer, when it comes to marketing myself, I've found it similarly difficult to do. There are, however, several perspectives that have helped me work on it more effectively.

I strive to see my achievements as statements of fact instead of points of bragging. If I am informing my leadership about what I have done, then it feels less like boasting and more like educating. Going even further, if I connect what I've done to end results and impact, I feel that I'm discussing how I've made a difference and not merely glowing about what a good worker I've been. I'm showing how I have served the company's mission by improving its bottom line.

It might seem crazy to employ such mind games, but women constantly tell me how awkward they feel about talking about themselves. As a result, their brand, an amazing brand, sits on the shelf unnoticed. All of us, it seems, need to become more tactfully assertive.

## WHO'S TALKING ABOUT YOU?

The big brands realize that word-of-mouth selling is the real end goal. A great brand strategy focuses on getting everyone talking about the brand in similar yet personalized ways. Consider the following examples:

- "Target has cool things for great prices" (general brand attribute).
- "I bought a set of twelve crystal glasses to use at Christmas, and they look like a million bucks" (personalized experience).

- "Cathy is a creative genius" (general brand attribute).
- "She recently developed our Asia product distribution strategy" (personalized experience).

92

Who are the people you want talking about you? Do they have enough facts and impressions to consistently say similar things? Do they have enough personal encounters to back up the facts with actual, measurable experiences?

Tom Peters is my favorite brand guru. His books are huge best sellers, and he has consulted with major companies the world over. He describes what we're talking about this way:

> Who are the people you want talking about you? Do they have enough facts and impressions to consistently say similar things?

> The key to any personal branding campaign is "word-of-mouth marketing." Your network of friends, colleagues, clients, and customers is the most important marketing vehicle you've got; what they say about you and your contributions are what the market will ultimately gauge as the value of your brand. So the big trick to building your brand is to find ways to nurture your network of colleagues—consciously.[8]

## PREPARE FOR PROMOTION WHILE BUILDING YOUR BRAND

Use the following chart to picture, plan, and produce actions that will lead to promotion and, at the same time, build your personal brand. Keep in mind that while our felt need is for promotion, our real need is to build our personal brands. If we build them actively and strategically, promotion will be the by-product.

While you are anticipating that next promotion or the opportunity you've been waiting for, keep in mind that every single day can be an investment in your most important asset of all: the brand called you. Instead of waiting for your "consumers" to find you on the shelf, invest your resources in picturing, planning, and then producing a consistent brand of choice in everything you do.

"If you're going to be a brand," Tom Peters advises, "you've got to become relentlessly focused on what you do that adds value, that you're proud of, and most important, that you can shamelessly take credit for."[9]

There is so much opportunity for all of us, right here and right now. Before, during, and after promotion, we can be occupied with gladness of heart. While we may not come to it naturally, we can certainly come to it proactively. And job satisfaction can be ours with an ever-increasing momentum rather than an up-and-down cycle of high hopes and low disappointments.

| Desired Brand Attribute (Picture) | Current Perception and Gaps I Must Address (Plan) | Action Steps to Improve and Build Desired Brand (Produce) |
|---|---|---|
| *Example 1:* Being recognized as an innovator in the area of customizing careers | Seen as a "doer" but not a "thinker" | 1. Research who in my company is an expert.<br>2. Research who outside the company is considered the guru on this topic.<br>3. Send an e-mail to the in-house expert inquiring about ways to get more involved in the strategy aspects of what our company is doing in career customization.<br>4. Attend a conference where the guru is speaking. |
| *Example 2:* Being assigned as a team leader for a high-profile project | Considered too crucial for current project to be given any others | 1. Talk to the current team leader about an exit strategy or a plan to delegate some of the work.<br>2. Get smart about the goals of the high-profile project and share ideas with that project's manager; this will create additional advocacy.<br>3. Put this idea into next year's goals form so broader leadership commitment can be garnered. |

Picture your ideal world. Plan your dream future. Produce every possibility you can think of or imagine. In short, it's time to follow the advice of one famous brand we all know. Just do it!

*I knew what I wanted to do and was done with it by age thirty. I'd been in the White House, in the diplomatic service, and influencing foreign policy. I wasn't just reading about it but was actually being part of it. Somewhat by accident I had a personal board.*

—CELINA REALUYO
Former Director for Counterterrorism,
U.S. Department of State

# SIX

# How Do I Get from "Great Idea" to "Dream Come True"?

S earch engines are a wonderful thing. When I want to find out anything about anything, any time of day, all I have to do is wander over to my laptop and type in a phrase, and seconds later I have hundreds of links to information and ideas I didn't even know existed.

Now imagine getting similar returns from real people—about yourself. The minute you realize you need something in any area of your life, you simply drop an e-mail or call the person you know is a well-versed expert. Not only do they give you excellent information, but they tailor it just for you. They are focused on you, care about you, and are committed to you.

Not only do you have access to the insight of these individuals, but they also link you to their network of relationships, quite possibly the most powerful perk of this live "search engine."

## THE CHALLENGE: I NEED MORE HELP,
## INSPIRATION, AND CONNECTIONS

Renowned board expert John Carver estimated in his 1989 book, *Boards That Make a Difference*, that there were at that time approximately 4.5 million boards in the U.S. alone (nonprofit, governmental, and business). He notes, "It is virtually impossible to escape contact with boards. We either are on boards, work for them, or are affected by their decisions. Boards sit atop almost all corporate forms of organization—profit and non-profit—and often over governmental agencies as well."[1] The same certainly holds true today in greater numbers.

A few years back, I was having lunch with my friend Christie. I was feeling apathetic about my work. She was new to the company and not quite sure how to sort through the myriad projects, people, and priorities in order to be sure to get to her promised results.

We were on a creative flow in our conversation, imagining how to get further down the path toward our respective dreams, when she started encouraging me to think about the people I knew who were experts in the areas of my biggest dreams.

The longer we talked, the more people I recalled. These were individuals who could be great resources of insight, creative talent, and the influence I needed to move forward in becoming a more widely known, well-paid motivational speaker (something that was high on my aspirations list but not in my job description at the time).

> I wondered why I wouldn't have my own personal board, focused entirely on my dreams. It was an interesting way to approach what I needed at the time.

"It's like you need your own personal board of directors, Lynette," she said, "people who can help you become educated and connected in order to actually achieve this dream."

I was intrigued by the concept of a personal board, having worked with boards for many years in the nonprofit world. I had been a board member, the president of a board, and an executive director reporting to a board. I attended seminars and taught seminars on effective board leadership.

## How Do I Get From "Great Idea" to "Dream Come True"?

So I wondered why I wouldn't have my own personal board, focused entirely on my dreams. It was an interesting way to approach what I needed at the time. I spent the next few weeks thinking about recruiting and forming my personal board.

If I was going to be a speaker, I needed to know more clearly what the pay structure is, how to get my name out in the market, how to determine speaking topics, and how to effectively solicit speaking engagements. I organized in my mind and on paper an outline for several committees that would help me find the answers I needed. I thought through which questions needed to be asked.

My initial board plan looked something like this:

| Committee | What I Need to Know | Potential Commitee Members | Action Steps |
|---|---|---|---|
| Speaker Committee | How do I get started? How do I structure my fees? How do I determine my topics? How do I get bookings? What about products to sell? | Jim Stovall Bob Harrison | E-mail Jim and set up a time to talk. Have my sister ask Chris and Michelle if Bob might want me to speak at his Hawaii event. |
| Web Site Committee | Who could help create a Web site? What content do I need? How do I get listed on search engines? | Jenni Frost Tim Frost | Talk to Jenni about Tim to see if he has the time to help me get started. Set up a time with Jenni's photographer to get photos taken for the Web site. |

| Committee | What I Need to Know | Potential Commitee Members | Action Steps |
|---|---|---|---|
| Products and Branding Committee | What speaking content do I have that could be turned into a product? What kind of products should I have? What look and feel should my materials have? I need a logo. | Carol Spann<br><br>Dean Butler | Talk to Carol about these ideas and get her input. Call Dean and see if he can design a logo, get cost estimate. |
| Finance and Legal Committee | How much is all this going to cost? Where can I readjust my budget? Do I need to set up a separate company? | Dad<br><br><br>Joel LaCourse | Once I get estimates from other committees, work with Dad to set up a financial structure. Talk to Joel about setting up a corporation. |

It was amazing how much energy and motivation I generated merely by putting together this board structure. Now, in addition to the busy, demanding hours I was keeping at Deloitte, I was investing every free moment I could to talk to my new board members (most of whom never even knew they'd been nominated or recruited).

I remember the first thirty-minute phone meeting I set up with Jim Stovall, a good friend and founder of the Emmy-award-winning Narrative Television Network. Jim is a well-known, highly paid speaker, and at his suggestion, I called him at 7:00 one morning with my list of questions prepared.

I took pages of notes as fast as my pen would write. Jim talked about many ideas that related to the goals I shared. By the time we finished, I had several pages of ideas to pursue, along with Jim's enthusiasm and commitment to help me. "Any time you ever need anything, Lynette, just let me know," he offered.

Over the next few weeks, I began moving forward on several of Jim's ideas. Meanwhile, I was also talking to the others on my various committees. In two months, I was invited by Bob Harrison, another one of my Speaker Committee members, to speak for his leader's conference in Maui in February. It would coincide with my fortieth birthday, so several family members decided they would also attend. (I really had to twist their arms!)

Preparing for this exciting event provided further motivation and direction for my planning. I knew I'd need some products to sell, so I used weekends to write my first instructional manual on building purpose-focused teams. This topic would become an area of recognized expertise and focus in ensuing years.

I found a recording studio on 23rd Street in Manhattan and took in two of my best speaking tapes for editing. I would market and sell them at the conference.

Dean Butler, from my Products and Branding Committee, worked with me to create a beautiful logo that I printed on business cards and note cards (the ones I still use today). We came up with a look and image for the products I was pulling together.

Tim Frost, from my Web Site Committee, took Dean's graphics and put them up on my new Web site. The site was simple, but it had enough information that I could list it on my new business cards and point people to it for more information.

By the time the Hawaii event rolled around, I had three beautiful products to sell, a logo and identity materials, and a Web site. At the end of my presentation, I had several more speaking engagements and I sold out of all my materials. What an encouragement! I was on my way.

Once again, there was nothing in my job description at Deloitte that gave me permission or assignment to move ahead with my board or these dreams. I made sure nothing I was doing would go against company policy, and my boss knew I was exploring new ways to speak more frequently and add credentials to my résumé.

I credit my board of directors for helping ignite and launch these ideas. I have since identified new board members and retired some initial ones, but all the while I found tremendous motivation and encouragement from this organized approach to identifying the people and resources I most need to help me get to the next places I want to go.

## THE STRATEGY: ORGANIZE A PERSONAL
## BOARD OF DIRECTORS

**What pictures of promotion are in your mind, and who do you need to help you get there?**

What if right now, today, you organized your own board of directors? What pictures of promotion are in your mind, and who do you need to help you get there? Use the same chart I used and begin to explore and dream about whom you can call upon to serve your vision and dreams, even without their taking official or obligatory positions.

Jot in this chart some initial names and ideas to get your juices flowing. Be sure to include the action items that will help you get started. Then let your personal board help you to the next level.

| Committee | What I Need to Know | Potential Commitee Members | Action Steps |
|---|---|---|---|
| | | | |
| | | | |
| | | | |
| | | | |

## IDENTIFYING BOARD MEMBERS

The categories on the chart will provide enough information for you to understand why and how you want to approach your board members for help. Keep in mind, you never even have to mention your board. Naming this group of people is just a creative way of helping organize your need for experts and support in working toward your bigger dreams.

In his book *Extraordinary Board Leadership*, business expert Doug Eadie describes what he calls "high-impact boards." He says that such board members bring to the boardroom their experience, expertise, knowledge, skills, and networks of association. High-impact board members make a measurable impact on an organization's resources, performance, and influence.[2]

This is an excellent guide for a personal board as well. Your members will make a significant impact by helping you identify resources, improve your personal performance, and broaden your influence.

> Your members will make a significant impact by helping you identify resources, improve your personal performance, and broaden your influence.

Celina Realuyo, who is formerly the director for counterterrorism in the U.S. Department of State, has experienced firsthand the measurable impact of her own personal board of directors. In a recent conversation, she described how her personal board helped her achieve many of her goals very early in her career.

> I knew what I wanted to do and was done with it by age thirty. I'd been in the White House, in the diplomatic service, and influencing foreign policy. I wasn't just reading about it but was actually being part of it. Somewhat by accident I had a personal board.

## EVALUATING BOARD MEMBER CONTRIBUTIONS

When you are evaluating potential board members, consider three categories of contribution that a typical individual can make.

1. *Time.* Does this person have time for engaging in discussions, sorting and planning, and working on projects with you and for you?
2. *Talent.* Does this person have a specific talent, craft, or skill that you need to progress further on certain goals?
3. *Treasure.* Is this person able to invest in you by giving money or bartering services that you would otherwise have to pay for?

On my Web Site Committee right now, for example, I have one person whom I utilize for his tremendous expertise and overall vision in the area of Web design. He has great talent but not much time to actually help execute the Web site content, updates, and ongoing evolution of my site. Another committee member is in between jobs, so she has extra time to invest in the execution of the vision and updates to the site but limited experience in overall Web strategy. I need both of them on my committee but for different reasons—one for talent, one for time.

Occasionally you'll find board members with more than one category to offer. It is terrific when you do, but realize that more often than not, your members will only be able to offer one.

I spent several years of frustration with board members (not my personal board but the other boards with whom I worked). There were those who would show up to every single meeting but never contribute a dime to the fund-raising efforts. Or others who would write large checks but missed two out of every three meetings. When I learned about the time, talent, and treasure measures, I began to more deeply appreciate each board member, realizing that I could celebrate their unique contributions without complaining about what they could not or would not give.

## APPROACHING PERSONAL BOARD MEMBERS

Having outlined the committees you need and considered the time, talent, and treasure you are looking for, you are ready to approach your personal board members.

Those whom you know well and already have a strong relationship with are generally easy to approach for specific help or input. People whom you don't yet know or those in more senior positions who are extremely busy and hard to get time with may require some forethought. Here are a few key points to remember as you approach them:

## How Do I Get From "Great Idea" to "Dream Come True"?

*What skills are they most proud of?* Most everyone is pleased about something they've accomplished. Think about the person you are approaching, and affirm those things that have personally satisfied them the most. Keep in mind these may not be work related. The CEO of the giant software distributor may be most proud of the athletic achievements of his son who has Down syndrome. You might approach him as your board member for insights on volunteering in the community instead of the obvious role of strategist for your developing software ideas.

*What can you offer in return?* In his book *The Irresistible Offer*, Mark Joyner proposes, "Business simply does not get done—in fact, it doesn't even start—until an offer is made. The core imperative of business is simply this: Make an offer."[3] Even though you are asking potential board members for something, consider what you can offer in return. My friend Dean, board member for my personal branding initiatives, was just launching his own business, and it turned out that my materials would be useful for his own growing portfolio.

*Be specific and succinct when you're requesting help.* Busy people with lots of talent are likely to be your first choice recruits for your personal board. The way to gain their time, treasure, or talent is to be very specific and succinct in what you are requesting.

### ACKNOWLEDGING THEIR EFFORTS

When busy people are generous enough to give you something, such as time, a letter of recommendation, or ideas for your next big venture, never forget to acknowledge them. Do it in a creative way that is memorable and means something to them personally.

My mentor Carole Hyatt collects matchstick holders, a tie-in to what she has spent her entire career doing—matching people with new opportunities. In her living room she has many beautiful holders people have sent her from all over the world in appreciation for her helping them find a great match.

I once wrote a letter of recommendation for a friend who was applying to law school. Just days after I sent it, she sent me a box of high-end steaks. We remembered her thoughtfulness every time we fired up the grill.

Gabriela Ferrari, who works in the global business intelligence department of Nike, shared with me the following inspiring example of how she expressed appreciation to one of her personal board members:

There are many ways to say thank you—and one must do it, constantly. To me, the most important thing is that recognition is timely and *personal.*

I had been seeking a certain promotion for quite a while, and when it finally happened, I remembered a special member of my personal board who had taken time from her busy schedule to sit down with me and listen to challenges I was facing when designing my course of action months earlier. She is a beautiful African-American woman who heads global diversity, so I decided to buy the most beautiful and exuberant orchid I could find. I presented it to her along with a card that acknowledged her leadership and support, which were instrumental in making things happen. I explained the choice of orchids—beautiful and rare, just like her.

This simple act brought tears to her eyes. She told me that the card and orchid could not have arrived at a better time, one when she needed to hear that her efforts were making a difference.

This was a reminder that even the most successful and important people in the world need and like to hear that their contributions bring value into others' lives.[4]

While gifts are nice, we shouldn't diminish the power of a simple, personal, handwritten note. In an age of electronic mail, snail mail often comes as a pleasant and memorable surprise.

Florence Littauer, in her book *A Letter Is a Gift Forever,* reminds us of earlier days when the art of expressing thankfulness was taught to every lady. "In the early years of the 20th century it was considered part of a young woman's training to learn how to write a proper thank you note. As a part of social graces each girl was groomed to have polite manners, sit properly, embroider pillowcases, and write thank you notes on the correct paper with the proper pen."[5]

> **While gifts are nice, we shouldn't diminish the power of a simple, personal, handwritten note.**

While I may not always use the "correct" paper and pen, I have diligently worked on this skill of expressing gratitude frequently, personally, and creatively to the point of making it a component of my personal brand. I see it as a deposit into those whom I value and appreciate.

Giving acknowledgment in ways that speak deeply to someone's heart is an art you *can* learn and, I propose, we all *should* learn, as we often receive valuable gifts from others who deserve our heartfelt appreciation.

There are some excellent books on this topic, including the one mentioned above by Florence Littauer, and another one of my favorites, *Gift of a Letter* by Alexandra Stoddard.[6] Both authors emphasize that any handwritten note is a small gift in itself, one we all love to receive yet seldom take the time to give.

There are a few guidelines that I keep in mind when I am expressing my gratitude in writing to my board members, or for that matter, anyone I appreciate.

*Make it about them.* Rather than emphasize yourself ("I so appreciate what you have given"), focus on the giver. You could write, "The time you invested by phone this morning was truly a gift; you are so generous, and I am sincerely grateful."

*Be specific.* Rather than expressing, "Working with you has given me so much," tell them exactly what you received. "Your ideas about contacts for the research prompted an immediate call to Suzanne Behr, who provided even further connections with two industry experts."

*Highlight the difference they made.* When we invest our resources of time, talent, and treasure, we are glad to know how the investment paid off. When you are expressing your appreciation for such an investment into you, highlight this return on investment for your investors. Rather than saying, "Your efforts made such a difference," go with something like, "I would not have found the answers I needed without your generous insights and encouragement. I have four new workshops planned because of the advice you offered."

> Think about a new area of interest, and identify two or three people who could add tremendous ideas, connections, and inspiration to help you pursue it further.

If these hints remind you of a thank-you that should have been written but wasn't, take time to write it now. We hear stories of teachers who hear from their former students years later about the impact they made on the students' lives. What a gift that can be, no matter how many years have passed.

Florence Littauer reminds us of this. "A letter of thanks is never overdue," she writes, "even though seasons pass, lives change, memories fade. The words of a dear one will go back in time and acknowledge the thank yous that were once forgotten."[7]

Our lives are so busy and the tasks at hand often so demanding that taking even small steps in the direction of our dreams is often a challenge. A personal board of directors is one concrete, practical tool for leveraging relationships in a way that is rewarding for them and invaluable for you.

If the thought of forming an entire personal board is too daunting, begin with one committee. Think about a new area of interest, and identify two or three people who could add tremendous ideas, connections, and inspiration to help you pursue it further.

Not long ago, I was teaching this idea of creating a personal board to a group of corporate women. One of them mentioned her interest in traveling to Europe and said that it was something she had wanted to do for years. She was extremely busy, however, and was consequently having a hard time moving this desire from dream to reality.

> Do yourself the favor of more effectively leveraging all those people you know or want to know in a structured, motivating way.

She decided to set up a European Exploration Committee. She was excited as she shared with the group how this committee would help her research and plan her first visit. Her dream was not specifically work related, but it enhanced her work by giving herself permission to make room for something that mattered deeply to her on a more personal level. Interestingly, as she began planning, she realized there were people in her workplace who could be part of the committee, contributing to and enhancing her dream.

While I have not heard if she has taken her trip, I can only imagine how much fun she has had continuing to dream and plan, not to mention the interesting people she has talked to and ideas she's discovered, all from simply organizing this one new committee.

Now it is your turn. Where will you begin? Starting with one seed of an idea can help you begin forming first a committee, then later a board. What fun it is to rally these resources toward our most important plans and dreams. It takes more time than the typical search engine, but like those engines, this search yields a wealth of surprising information and resources we never even knew existed.

Do yourself the favor of more effectively leveraging all those people you know or want to know in a structured, motivating way. You'll move a few steps closer to the people you admire and the resources your dreams need.

*Every year I use the same illustration. I give each player a stick and have them decorate it. Then I gather up all the sticks and give each person's stick to someone else. I tell them, "Take the stick in your hands and break it." At first they are a bit upset. "We just spent time decorating these sticks." "Break it in half." Then I give them a piece of tape and have them tape it back together again.*

—SYLVIA HATCHELL
University of North Carolina
head women's basketball coach,
two-time AP Coach of the Year

# SEVEN

# Can I Really Thrive in Leadership?

**E**arly in our careers, few of us list "being a great leader" as one of our goals. Leadership roles tend to sneak up on us, and suddenly others are looking at us, hoping to find reasons to follow our lead.

Max Depree, one of my favorite authors on leadership, fittingly calls leadership an art. In his book *Leadership Is an Art*, he offers insight that helped cultivate my own leadership theories early in my career.

> People are the heart and spirit of all that counts. Without people, there is no need for leaders. Leaders can decide to be primarily concerned with leaving assets to their institutional heirs or they can go beyond that and capitalize on the opportunity to leave a legacy, a legacy that takes into account the more difficult, qualitative side of life, one which provides greater meaning, more challenge, and more joy in the lives of those whom leaders enable.[1]

Helping those I lead to find joy, as Max says, has become one of my primary goals as a leader. It has become a way of achieving my broader life purpose. It has taken time to cultivate the skills to do it well, but the cultivation process itself has been surprisingly rewarding.

## THE CHALLENGE: I NEED TO LEAD IN A WAY THAT MAXIMIZES PEOPLE'S PASSION AND POTENTIAL

The process of becoming a great leader is not for the fainthearted. Still, I find it encouraging to know that leadership skills can be learned and are not reserved for the naturally talented few.

Leadership expert Warren Bennis, who has consulted with four U.S. presidents and more than 150 CEOs and written twenty-seven books on the topic of leadership, offers the following encouragement: "The most dangerous leadership myth is that leaders are born—that there is a genetic factor to leadership. This myth asserts that people simply either have certain charismatic qualities or not. That's nonsense; in fact, the opposite is true. Leaders are made rather than born."

> If leadership is an art and we don't have to be born a leader, everyone should aspire to leadership in some way—even if only to better lead ourselves.

If leadership is an art and we don't have to be born a leader, everyone should aspire to leadership in some way—even if only to better lead ourselves.

I will always remember my first formal experience in leadership. After many years of working with only a loyal band of faithful volunteers, I was finally in a position to lead a staff of three people. I did not know how to manage or lead per se, and the organization I was in did not provide a collection of tools, processes, or standards to use.

For a while I plugged along and experimented. I would have weekly group meetings because it seemed like the thing to do. I met with each of my team members to encourage each person because encouragement was what came most naturally to me.

One young woman on my team was not very responsive to my style of leader-

114

ship. It was quite clear she wanted to be the leader and do it her way. I would hear through the office grapevine her sentiments on the matter: "Lynette is a type A person and I'm not. She just wants me to be like her." In reality, I just wanted her to be the type who would take constructive input and be led. But still, her criticisms played right into insecurities I had about my own liabilities. I was at a loss for what to do with her and in general.

Several of my girlfriends were in similar new leadership roles at the time. We would often talk about the challenges of leading and managing people, eventually having the fortuitous idea of meeting every other week for breakfast to focus more proactively on ways to grow in our leadership abilities.

Carol, Michelle, Gayle, Andrea, and I would meet for breakfast every other Wednesday morning at Rick's Café American. We would each read a chapter of Stephen Covey's book *Principle-Centered Leadership* during the week prior to the meeting, then come together to discuss our insights and, most important, the experiences we were having at work.

Over cups of coffee and breakfast goodies, we would share our stories of what was working and not working with our various staff people. We would listen to one another's dilemmas and then brainstorm ways to improve outcomes and relationships. The collective wisdom of the group was a huge help.

I received so much from the meetings with these women, sometimes amid tears of frustration but always in the company of much wit and laughter. I see now that we were in essence mentoring one another. Even though we were basically at the same points in our careers and of similar ages, we each provided the others with insights and encouragement that made a lasting impact on the way we lead.

In the absence of mentors in my own organization, I was also tutored from the shelves of the business section of my local bookstore. I simply began to apply and experiment with what I was reading. When Peter Drucker talked about the ideal length of time for meetings, I stuck to the clock and learned how to organize an agenda effectively and efficiently.[2]

When Laurie Beth Jones wrote about the importance of each person matching their mission to the company's mission, I put together a team-building day that would help each of us understand our unique role on the team, our strengths and weaknesses, and how to work together with greater power and commitment to one another.[3]

During the course of the next ten years, still waiting for my own ideal leader to emerge and mentor me, I kept forming and fashioning my own tools, theories, and techniques for leadership. Some worked brilliantly and became part of my tool kit. Others flopped miserably or wouldn't work for certain personalities.

My staff grew to include more people, and each new person helped hone my skills even further. I found that while managing people is extremely time intensive, when done well it yields a satisfaction and sense of reward unlike other duties of the job.

I could actually see people's lives grow richer. I watched their faces light up as they began to see their dreams move from far-off ideas to top-of-mind components of their daily work. The staff meetings shifted from drudgery to weekly highlights. The individual meetings became more powerful. Over the course of a decade, the reading, mentoring, and commitment to develop my skills brought forth confidence in managing and leading people, individually and as a team.

## THE STRATEGY: IMPLEMENT CREATIVE TOOLS THAT MAXIMIZE EVERYONE ON THE TEAM

One of the most successful leaders I know is Sylvia Hatchell. She is the head women's basketball coach at the University of North Carolina, Chapel Hill. She has spent her thirty-one-year career teaching talented young women how to grow and become great not only individually but also as a team.

I spoke with her the day after she won the Associated Press Coach of the Year for the second time. Clearly she knows a lot about leadership. She shared with me how she teaches her teams about teamwork.

Constantly I talk to my players about team building, teamwork, and unity. They are all great players, but their success is multiplied ten times over when they are working with each other.

Every year I use the same illustration. I give each player a stick and have them decorate it. Then I gather up all the sticks and give each person's stick to someone else. I tell them, "Take the stick in your hands and break it." At first they are a bit upset. "We just spent time decorating these sticks." "Break it in half." Then I give them a piece of tape and have them tape it back together again.

I'll say, "Now look, it doesn't matter what the newspaper says, what your mommy and daddy say about how great you are. When you're out there alone,

116

you can be easily broken; you are vulnerable." Then I take all the sticks, which are now all taped back together. One by one I put each person's stick into a bunch. I'll say, "Now Camille's stick is in the middle of the bunch; someone break it," and of course they can't.

"You are not as good alone as you are all together. Let's say one of you gets mad so you go off by yourself." I pull one stick out of the bunch and throw it aside, then throw another one out. "Now when you go off alone, you can be broken. But also, consider what you have now done to the core; you've made it weaker also. You have to trust each other no matter what."

Before every game we pass that group of sticks around the locker room. Then we take it into the game, where it stays by my chair until the last buzzer, reminding us that more than anything else, we are a team.[4]

While Sylvia's job as head coach implicitly involves building a team, every leader is challenged with team building, whether our teams are formed by job description or brought together around specific projects or shared goals.

> Every leader is challenged with team building, whether our teams are formed by job description or brought together around specific projects or shared goals.

Renowned leadership expert John C. Maxwell, in his book *The 360 Degree Leader*, explains today's imperative. "Productive leaders understand that one is too small a number to achieve greatness. . . . In the 2000s, the idea is team leadership. Because leading an organization has become so complex and multifaceted, the only way to make progress is to develop a team of leaders. I think organizations are going to improve greatly as they develop teams, because leadership is so complex. You can't just do one thing well and be a good leader. You can't even lead in just one direction—you need the skills to lead up, across, and down!"[5]

In twenty-two years of working with employees and managing teams, I have found three tools that have proven to be so highly effective in motivating my various teams that I do not lead or manage a group without them. I have personally used these with both small and large staffs, nonprofit boards and volunteers. I have taught them to many other leaders through seminars and workshops, occasionally serving as a facilitator for groups not quite ready to implement them on their own.

One such group was from a large pharmaceutical company with corporate offices in New Jersey. We spent a day together at an off-site location, focusing first on their personal purposes, then moving into team-building exercises, finishing with both individual and team strategies for helping each person better leverage their skills and interests around the company's primary goals. They were invigorated and excited about new possibilities they discovered that day, both as individuals and as a team. I have heard from a couple of them since who have said they are pleasantly surprised at how the lessons from that day remain with them several years later.

For business owners and those involved in network marketing companies (a growing trend that provides a unique mix of entrepreneurial fulfillment, team building, and the flexibility of working where and when you want), these tools can save many hours. Though simple to understand and implement, they consistently yield exciting results.

## TOOL#1: THE TEAM-BUILDING DAY

> A team-building day is an inventive way to get people to step away from their daily pressures and focus on how their individual purpose fits into broader corporate goals.

A team-building day is an inventive way to get people to step away from their daily pressures and focus on how their individual purpose fits into broader corporate goals. This day, just once or twice a year, can effectively create mutual understanding of one another's desires and dreams and teach the team how to more successfully work together toward common business goals.

There are many ways to organize such a day. The sample agenda that follows is one I have tested numerous times with great results.

## TEAM-BUILDING DAY
## SAMPLE AGENDA

| Time | Activity | Deliverable | Logistics |
|---|---|---|---|
| *Morning* | *Getting to Know Our Team* | | |
| 8:00–9:00 | Commute to location | N/A | Rent van—Diane to arrange; let team know when and where to meet |
| 9:00–9:30 | Everyone arrives<br><br>Continental breakfast | N/A | Sandra to arrange for breakfast foods—bagels and muffins, fruit platter, Krispy Kremes; Lynette will have coffees, juices, and milk; Sandra to supplement anything Lynette needs |
| 9:30–10:00 | Welcome from (leader)<br><br>Goals for the day | List of goals for the day posted on flip chart | Flip chart and markers, masking tape, several white notepads—Sandra to arrange |
| 10:00–11:30 (8 people, 8–10 minutes each) Will take a brief break when necessary | Self-disclosure: presentation of gift bag contents: everyone shares what's in their bags and why; people can ask questions of one another | Understanding one another's backgrounds, hobbies, interests | Get shopping bags from Bergdorf's—Winnie will get from friend<br><br>Do instruction sheet for activity—Lynette to draft; Sandra to print and organize with bags |

119

# Climbing the Ladder in Stilettos

| Time | Activity | Deliverable | Logistics |
|---|---|---|---|
| 11:30–12:30 | Strengths and weaknesses: each person shares about one weakness in their work life; others go around the circle and share a strength they see in that person | Person to the right of each presenter takes notes of all positive strength comments and gives to the person afterward | Winnie to bring colored note cards and envelopes |
| 12:30–1:00 | **Lunch** | N/A | Pizza from Domino's being delivered; Christine will get the drinks; Sandra to supplement what Lynette needs |
| *Afternoon* | *Purpose/Goals/Visions* | | |
| 1:00–1:30 | Each person states a goal or two they have for their personal or professional life | Lays the groundwork for team goals | Individual notes as desired |
| 1:30–3:00 | Identity and core service offerings: Who is (organization) today, next year, five years? Financial goals: today, next year, five years | Discussion of corporate purpose, our vision, our offerings, clients we want to pursue, our strengths and weaknesses as a group, awards and recognition we want to pursue | Flip charts, someone assigned to take notes or to enter ideas on a laptop |
| 3:00–3:15 | **Break** | | Cheese, crackers, fruit—Sandra to arrange |

| Time | Activity | Deliverable | Logistics |
|---|---|---|---|
| 3:15–3:45 | Individual purpose Roles and responsibilities | Based on team goals, discussion of our individual purpose and what roles are necessary, who is best at what roles, how work roles support earlier stated purpose, goals and strengths | Same |
| 3:45–4:00 | Benefits: What other things do we need to thrive? | Understanding extra activities to be added to budget (i.e., what type of training, field trips, fun?) | Same |
| 4:00–4:30 | Values and attributes | As we work toward goals, what values will we commit to and embrace along the way, with our clients and with one another? | Same |
| 4:30–6:00 | Adjourn, clean up, drive back to office | | |
| 6:30–8:30 | Dinner | Reflection on day, fun | Sandra to make reservations at Genarro, on the Upper West Side |

Many organizations spend lots of money and hire outside consultants to facilitate this type of team-building day. Having been part of many of these sessions through the years and facilitating many of my own, I have found that this agenda, when facilitated by the team leader (ideally) or someone else with facilitation skills on the team, brings stronger results without a huge investment.

In conjunction with the agenda above, here are a few pointers on the components involved in making such a day a success.

*Size of the team.* The size of each team will vary, and the team-building day can be adapted to any number of people. For maximum results, I find the ideal size to be five to eight people. This allows everyone to actively participate and interact. For teams or groups that exceed this size, I recommend splitting up the team into smaller units of five to eight people for each day and having the highest-ranking team member in the entire group attend all team-building days to serve as a link and ensure that common discussion points are included across all sessions. A summary session back at the office is also worthwhile so that each group can debrief the broader team about their experiences and so that a collective understanding of purpose can be defined and articulated.

*Scheduling.* The team-building day should be scheduled far enough in advance to ensure that everyone on the team is present. This may be a challenge depending on the size of the team and whether others can cover the work during the time away. Nonetheless, it is crucial that each person on the team participates, even if that means hiring a temp to provide coverage back at the office.

> When people are discussing the important whys of life, the environment is a key element in enhancing the process.

*Location and timing.* The ideal team-building day is held off-site, somewhere comfortable and away from the daily grind. I typically host my teams at my home since I find a personal residence to be hard to beat in terms of comfort and relaxation. Not every team leader will feel comfortable doing this, and other alternatives are limitless. They can include a lodge or resort, a suites hotel, or even outdoors (for example, I held a portion of one team-building day in Central Park). The point here is that the location should be relaxing and comfortable, without tables and other furniture that tend to imply work. When people are discussing the important whys of life, the environment is a key element in enhancing the process.

The day typically begins at the usual work start time or perhaps a bit later, depending on drive time to the location. One full workday works best to allow for adequate discussion and interaction. On occasion I have attempted to squeeze the agenda into less time and find that it significantly compromises the intended outcomes. The agenda as it is outlined is a tested mix of personal development, corporate visioning, and practical exercises that build the team in a purpose-focused way.

*Role of the leader.* If you are the manager or leader of your team, then I recommend that you personally facilitate the session if you can. Not every leader is comfortable or equipped for this type of role, and if you are not, you can ask someone on your team to assist in facilitating while you actively participate in the rest of the day's exercises. It is essential that those you lead see you being honest and open during the self-disclosure exercises and know you are listening to them in an effort to build trust and rapport among everyone on the team.

## COMPONENTS OF TEAM-BUILDING DAY

*Self-disclosure exercise.* The agenda for the team-building day begins with a "get to know one another" exercise. This exercise requires some advance work on the part of each participant. Even groups with a long history of working together find this exercise to be enlightening, moving, and fun. Each team member is given a paper bag and told to fill it with items that represent who they are. They can make something like a collage or box that is unique for this exercise or simply pull together a collection of items to use in sharing who they are with the group. It is surprising how much creativity can abound in this exercise.

One individual I know baked sugar cookies that he cut and decorated in the shape of items that showcased his favorite things, such as an airplane and flowers and the Eiffel Tower. Another woman brought ingredients for a salad and explained how each ingredient was representative of a component of her life. She had written a "recipe for success," which she read as she mixed up her salad, which was then served for lunch. On the next page are instructions that can be handed out to attendees prior to the day.

## SPECIAL INSTRUCTIONS
## FOR GIFT BAG SELF-DISCLOSURE EXERCISE
(Distribute this instruction sheet one week prior to Team-Building Day)

Next week, we will be conducting our team-building day at (location). One of the goals of this day is to get to know each team member on a more personal level than usually afforded us in the typical office environment.

In preparation for the first exercise of the team-building day, please fill a simple shopping bag with items that will help the rest of us learn to know you better. You can fill this bag with a collection of existing items, such as photos, awards, favorite keepsakes, or anything already in your possession that represents what you want us to know about you. Or you may want to create something completely new for this exercise, such as a collage or a collection of phrases that explains more about who you are.

Others who have done this exercise have baked cookies in shapes of things they enjoy, filled the bag with shoes that each exemplify an aspect of who they are, sung a song and read a poem they composed about their lives, and so forth. The goal here is to be creative, recognizing that even what you select and how you present it will help us learn to know you more.

You will have about eight minutes to share your bag and explain its contents. Have fun, and enjoy the process of preparing for this team-building day.

## Can I Really Thrive in Leadership?

*Strengths and weaknesses.* Working on a common purpose is almost impossible without a high level of trust among the team. This second component of the day is intended to build trust and unity in the group through a simple but powerful exercise.

Each person is asked to describe one weakness in his or her life. It might be a tendency to overreact under pressure or to be fearful in the face of something new. After briefly describing the weakness, everyone else takes turns stating a strength they see in that person while someone in the group captures it all in writing.

When articulating a person's strength, the speaker should look directly at the person and say it to him or her instead of saying it in general to the group. For instance, instead of saying, "What I like about Cathy is how she takes time to really listen to people," the person speaking would say, "Cathy, what I appreciate about you is that you take the time to really listen to people."

The reason this is such a powerful exercise is that it begins with what most of us frequently do, which is identify our weaknesses. No matter how strong someone might appear, we all grapple with feelings of inadequacy. In contrast, when we hear someone describe a weakness that we have observed and find irritating, we become more compassionate by realizing that they themselves recognize it. When we follow weaknesses with statements of affirmation, suddenly, like every Super Bowl championship team knows, we begin guarding one another's weaknesses and making a way for one another's strengths. Every time I use this exercise, it has tremendous impact and builds a level of trust that remains long after that day.

*Purpose and mission.* This third component of the day typically begins after lunch and addresses purpose and mission. To begin, each person is asked to state one or two goals they have for their personal or professional life in the next year. They should keep this to one minute or two. If your team members have written a purpose statement as outlined in chapter 1, this is the time to share it with the group, along with the one or two goals.

The discussion then moves to the goals of the team. This can begin with an overview of the organization's purpose and mission, followed by a discussion of the team's purpose and mission within that organizational mission. The team leader should prepare much of this content ahead of time and use this component to solicit input and feedback and to achieve buy-in for the common purpose and goals. It is helpful to capture this discussion on flip charts or in some other way that team members can refer to it later in the discussion.

*Individual purpose and roles and responsibilities.* Now that the corporate purpose and mission are understood, and on the basis of earlier exercises that helped everyone understand the gifts and talents of individual team members, it is time to articulate each individual's purpose as related to their role at work.

This is where every person begins to see more clearly how their background, skills, strengths, and personal purpose and goals equip them uniquely for their role on the team.

*Values and attributes.* One other component that is a fitting end to the day includes a discussion of the values and attributes that the team wants to be recognized for in the broader organization. This list should be fairly short and comprised of those attributes that are most motivating to the way the team works together going forward. One team of marketing professionals I worked with chose the following attributes: strategic, indispensable, and embodying excellence. They wrote them down and posted them on their desks as ongoing reminders of the way they do business.

*Possible additional components.* The team-building day as outlined is a very full one-day agenda, but there may be other components you will want to develop on your own, tailored for your team and organization. For instance, the agenda includes a section on benefits that I have found to be useful in getting my teams to create a wish list for perks like training or field trips that they believe will enhance the pursuit of the broader purpose.

Feel free to adapt the proposed agenda as you wish while recognizing that the components, in the order recommended, have been widely tested and refined for desired results.

## TOOL #2: TEAM MEETINGS AND ONE-ON-ONES

In an ongoing effort to build a purpose-centered culture, I have found that full team meetings along with one-on-one meetings with key leaders are absolutely essential. In his classic book *The Effective Executive*, Peter Drucker explains it this way:

> To spend a few minutes with people is simply not productive. If one wants to get anything across, one has to spend a fairly large minimum quantum of time. The manager who thinks that he can discuss the plans, direction, and performance of

one of his subordinates in fifteen minutes—and many managers believe this—is just deceiving himself. If one wants to get to the point of having an impact, one needs probably at least an hour and usually much more.[6]

Full staff meetings, along with individual one-on-ones, demand an invest-ment of time but are key to ensuring that the energy and momentum from the team-building day are incorporated into the daily culture of the organization. I meet regularly with the key leaders of my team, and they in turn meet with their key leaders. In some cases these meetings are held weekly and in other cases every two weeks. The level of motivation and focus for the team tends to exponentially diminish with a frequency less than every two weeks.

Frequency can be somewhat varied, depending on the level of interaction that takes place daily among team members. This is especially true for global corporations, in which teams may be spread across several countries.

One such global team leader is Gabriela Ferrari from Nike, who has worked with virtual teams around the world. She shares some of the unique challenges of team building in a global corporation.

As a team leader, your role is both facilitator and communicator to disseminate information and get results. You are challenged to motivate and you are also the glue that holds it together; you must continually be in contact with various team members around the world.

It is essential to tailor your approach to the cultural needs of the team. The IT world is very project-driven, so my teams work on high-profile and deadline-driven projects. There's never enough time to get everything done.

One aspect of the work ethic in the United States is that of being very deadline-oriented. Working against deadlines is a common motivator we assume is in place. So in global projects we have to be very careful about cultural differences. Different teams have varying approaches to things such as working on the weekends, putting in overtime, etc. For example, in Europe they don't work like we do. Their perspec-tive is typically, "My time is my time." So if you don't take these differences into consideration, you will lose team commitment.

For our Asian teams, on the other hand, we have to give them time to explain goals and put deadlines in between. They tend to be more consultative and process-oriented, are very punctual about deadlines, but their process is different. If you allow teams to exercise their own process, they will give you the results you need.

127

Trust is key to getting results. No team or organization is capable of doing what its people are not. We must constantly be engaging people—it is one of the primary leadership challenges in business today.[7]

> **Essential benefits are derived from meetings where everyone reports on their activities and where you as the leader can continue reminding them that even mundane activities are contributing to the broader purpose.**

Whether your team is down the hall or across the globe, essential benefits are derived from meetings where everyone reports on their activities and where you as the leader can continue reminding them that even mundane activities are contributing to the broader purpose.

This same affirmation of purpose should take place in the one-on-one meetings with key team leaders. This is a chance for you to listen privately to the activities and challenges of your direct reports while discussing and interacting with them about how these activities contribute to their personal goals and aspirations.

One memorable experience convinced me of the importance of this practice. I had four direct reports at the time and met with three of the four on a weekly basis. The fourth person was in charge of a very busy accounting department, and since he did not have much new information to report each week, I assumed he would find the one-on-one meetings repetitive and perhaps even frustrating in light of his time-sensitive workload.

What I did not know is that while my other three team members were getting tremendous motivation and encouragement in our weekly meetings, feeling a strong sense of purpose in their work, he was being courted by another company promising more opportunity and promotion.

He took the other job only to find out that it was not all he had hoped. Soon after joining this other company, he left to join the Peace Corps, still searching for a sense of purpose. This was a great lesson to me about recognizing the vital importance of regular one-on-one meetings in affirming and reminding each team member of the unique contributions he or she makes.

## HINTS FOR EFFECTIVE TEAM MEETINGS AND ONE-ON-ONES

Every team is different, and the content of meetings will vary greatly from team to team and person to person. Nevertheless, here are a few overarching principles to keep in mind for typical team meetings:

- Begin promptly and on time.
- Prepare an agenda.
- Ask each team member to prepare a brief summary (three to five minutes, more depending on their project load) of their current projects.
- Invite the group to dialogue and troubleshoot items as necessary, but don't allow one person to dominate the time.
- Allow time, even if it's brief, for voicing general questions and concerns.
- End the meeting when the scheduled finishing time is reached.

For individual one-on-ones, I let the employees set the agenda. I ask them to come with a brief list of what they would like to cover. I use this list to take notes for myself and keep it in a file. This file provides tremendous help at the end of the year when I need to recall details of their work and performance.

## TOOL#3: EMPLOYEE EVALUATIONS

As one of my favorite leaders once told me, "You have to *in*spect what you *ex*pect." Building a purpose-centered culture might start off with a big bang on a team-building day, but if mechanisms for measuring and evaluating progress are not incorporated, over the course of time the sense of purpose begins to fade. Team-building days and regular meetings will help keep purpose alive, but the employee evaluation process is the security lock. It lets each person know that individual performance is not only a good thing but an essential thing that will be recognized and rewarded year after year.

Large organizations usually have rigorous processes and tools for goal setting and evaluations. If yours does not, here are two

> **Team-building days and regular meetings will help keep purpose alive, but the employee evaluation process is the security lock.**

sample employee evaluations that can work well and incorporate language about purpose. These can be adapted to your own existing templates and become part of the biannual or annual evaluation process your organization uses.

## NOTES ON EMPLOYEE EVALUATIONS

- Purpose of evaluation is to provide both parties a private, focused chance to openly discuss their relationship and their mutual purpose and goals within the organization. Excellent chance to affirm employee's unique contribution and build their loyalty to the organization and the supervisor.
- Tell employees at the beginning of their employment that they will receive a six-month evaluation, yearly thereafter. Provide them with the form at that time so they will understand criteria.
- Do first evaluation at six months, then at first-year anniversary, yearly thereafter. Modify second evaluation slightly since logistical details likely will have been well established by that time. Focus more on visioning and expansion of employee's role and duties.
- Honesty and openness are critical with an underlying commitment to build mutual trust and loyalty.
- Supervisor fills out form; employee fills out form. Following evaluation, copies of both parties' forms are filed in employee file.
- Take employee out for a nice lunch at a private place. Allow at least two hours for lunch and evaluation process.
- Supervisor begins by reading criteria and indicates the level of evaluation. Employee states her level. Both read their comments.
- Supervisor should communicate openness to employee's feedback so both walk away from evaluation with complete understanding of each other's purpose and commitment to bettering the work environment and achieving personal goals.

**SAMPLE 1**
(Company Name)
*Employee Evaluation Report*


**EMPLOYEE EVALUATION REPORT**

Employee:

Position:

Supervisor:

For the period of:

Today's date:

|  | Excellent | Good | Fair | Poor |
|---|---|---|---|---|
| 1. Personal habits | ☐ | ☐ | ☐ | ☐ |

Comments: _____

| | | | | |
|---|---|---|---|---|
| 2. Attendance and punctuality | ☐ | ☐ | ☐ | ☐ |

Comments: _____

| | | | | |
|---|---|---|---|---|
| 3. Accepts responsibility | ☐ | ☐ | ☐ | ☐ |

Comments: _____

| | | | | |
|---|---|---|---|---|
| 4. Attitude | ☐ | ☐ | ☐ | ☐ |

Comments: _____

| | | | | |
|---|---|---|---|---|
| 5. Judgment | ☐ | ☐ | ☐ | ☐ |

Comments: _____

| | | | | |
|---|---|---|---|---|
| 6. Oral communication | ☐ | ☐ | ☐ | ☐ |

Comments: _____

131

|                                         | Excellent | Good | Fair | Poor |
|-----------------------------------------|-----------|------|------|------|
| 7. Written communication                | ☐ | ☐ | ☐ | ☐ |
| Comments: _____       | | | | |
| 8. Quality of work                      | ☐ | ☐ | ☐ | ☐ |
| Comments: _____       | | | | |
| 9. Relates to staff                     | ☐ | ☐ | ☐ | ☐ |
| Comments: _____       | | | | |
| 10. Relates to customers/clients        | ☐ | ☐ | ☐ | ☐ |
| Comments: _____       | | | | |
| 11. Receptive to instruction/criticism  | ☐ | ☐ | ☐ | ☐ |
| Comments: _____       | | | | |
| 12. Receptive to individual differences | ☐ | ☐ | ☐ | ☐ |
| Comments: _____       | | | | |

Employee's comments:

Supervisor's comments:

Please articulate in a sentence or two your personal purpose statement relative to this position.

Please list five qualities/characteristics you would like people to use when describing you in your current position.

## Can I Really Thrive in Leadership?

Please indicate your personal/professional goals for the next three years.

How can the position of (position title) be modified, expanded, or improved to better enhance the above stated goals?

Please indicate how the (title of the person evaluating) can improve her management style, inprove her means of communicating, and/or make other changes toward a more productive and positive work environment.

What is your vision for the position of (position title) over the next three years? How would you like to see the position develop, including expansion of current programs or addition of new ones?

**SAMPLE 2**
(Company Name)
*Employee Evaluation Report*

## ANNUAL REVIEW

Employee:

Position:

Supervisor:

For the period of:

Today's date:

|  | Excellent | Good | Fair | Poor |
|---|---|---|---|---|
| **GENERAL AND PERSONAL** | | | | |
| Commitment to company purpose and mission | ☐ | ☐ | ☐ | ☐ |
| Communication skills | | | | |
|   Written | ☐ | ☐ | ☐ | ☐ |
|   Oral | ☐ | ☐ | ☐ | ☐ |
| Professionally represents company to clients/customers | ☐ | ☐ | ☐ | ☐ |
| Works harmoniously | | | | |
|   With staff | ☐ | ☐ | ☐ | ☐ |
|   With volunteers | ☐ | ☐ | ☐ | ☐ |

# Can I Really Thrive in Leadership?

|  | Excellent | Good | Fair | Poor |
|---|---|---|---|---|
| **MANAGERIAL** | | | | |
| Plans, organizes, and coordinates programs | ☐ | ☐ | ☐ | ☐ |
| Attention to detail and follow-up | ☐ | ☐ | ☐ | ☐ |
| Assists committees by attending meetings, supplying data, mailing notices, etc. | ☐ | ☐ | ☐ | ☐ |
| Compiles reports and maintains records accurately | ☐ | ☐ | ☐ | ☐ |
| Keeps the director apprised of potential problems | ☐ | ☐ | ☐ | ☐ |
| Corresponds with volunteers to maintain their sense of allegiance to organization | ☐ | ☐ | ☐ | ☐ |
| **PROFESSIONAL** | | | | |
| Accepts suggestions and criticism and makes changes accordingly | ☐ | ☐ | ☐ | ☐ |
| Offers suggestions objectively | ☐ | ☐ | ☐ | ☐ |
| Familiar with bylaws and traditions of organization | ☐ | ☐ | ☐ | ☐ |
| Respects organizational structure and lines of communications | ☐ | ☐ | ☐ | ☐ |

## OVERALL COMMENTS ON ABOVE ITEMS
Please articulate your personal purpose relative to this position.

# Climbing the Ladder in Stilettos

Please describe your top three personal goals for the upcoming year.

Please describe your top three professional goals for the upcoming year.

What changes, if any, need to be made in your current job structure to better facilitate the achievement of your personal and professional purpose and goals?

In your work environment, what additional resources do you need to better fulfill your responsibilities (e.g., personnel, equipment, reallocation of time or duties, etc.)?

Describe your views on the current reporting structure and outline ways to improve communication.

Do you have any other suggestions, criticisms, or ideas that need to be discussed? If so, please describe.

There is no question that leading people is one of the most strenuous yet rewarding aspects of work. At the beginning of my career, I found it daunting; now twenty-two years later, I find it the single most rewarding element of all I have achieved.

One of my employees at Deloitte a number of years ago was a young man named Spencer Wood. He was obviously talented well beyond his job description yet working hard to find his place at the firm. He dove right into the team-building days and staff meetings. Our one-on-ones were motivating to both of us. Self-discoveries he made during those few years helped launch him into his bigger dreams of starting the Icebox Athlete mental skills and toughness training company for athletes—an endeavor that has brought him major success and a growing, global company. Spencer has told me, "Lynette, I can trace the seeds of this dream I'm living back to that time when I was part of your team. That season watered and cultivated my ideas, bringing me to a place of confidence where I could live my purpose in a more proactive way."

When I hear things like this, I'm reminded that the energy and time it takes to lead effectively are worth it, and I discover new motivation to be a model of what Peter Drucker suggests is great leadership: "Leadership is lifting a person's vision to high sights, the raising of a person's performance to a higher standard, the building of a personality beyond its normal limitations."[8]

> A leader is someone who finds surprising joy in life by celebrating the achievements of those she leads.

Armed with a few of the tools I've provided, or some of your own that work well for you, call yourself a leader no matter what stage you are in professionally. Don't worry about being perfect—remember, we grow as we lead. Read as much as you can from the experts, learning from their knowledge and mistakes. Become efficient and effective with even just a couple of tools; make them your own and part of your brand of leadership. Be willing to learn from those you lead. Ask them, "How am I doing?" and "What can I do better?"

At the end of the day, measure your impact as a leader not simply by what your team has achieved but by how every team member has grown as an individual. Reflect on it often, and in doing so you will give them yet one more lesson in leadership—a leader is someone who finds surprising joy in life by celebrating the achievements of those she leads.

*In today's global marketplace, there are greater communication challenges than ever before. This is something the American Dairy Association discovered when they decided to take their highly successful "Got Milk?" campaign to Mexico and found out that the Spanish translation read, "Are you lactating?"*

# EIGHT

# Who, Me? Speak in Public?

**I**f there is one ability that can open up more doors than anything else, it is the ability to speak with poise and confidence anytime, to anyone, anywhere.

We don't all speak in large, public ways, but all of us speak every day. Carla Kimball, who has been a public speaking executive coach for more than eighteen years, explained to me how important this skill can be.

> Public speaking requires the ability to speak up and to relate to others. It isn't just about standing in front of a podium and speaking to a large audience. It also means speaking up in meetings, communicating effectively with clients, and answering tough questions presented by a team of colleagues and superiors. It means being able to convey your ideas effectively on the telephone, one-on-one, and to small and large groups of people. It is the ability to influence and inspire others and to effect change.[1]

Not only is speaking a part of everyday life, but according to Patricia Fripp, the first female president of the more than four-thousand-member National Speaker's Association, speaking is a great way to add credibility to your business reputation.[2]

The fear of speaking before a group still ranks number one in top ten fears (ahead of heights, flying, and death).[3] In spite of the common fear of public speaking, there are ways to improve this all-important skill and leverage it more effectively as a tremendous business asset.

> Like many other business and personal skills, speaking is something that improves with practice. The more you do it, the better you get, and therefore the less you fear it as your confidence grows.

Carla was telling me recently about a young woman who was like many women who move up quickly in their carreers. They have positions of authority and are given opportunities to speak to, work with, and supervise people older than they are. As a result, these women often feel insecure when speaking. Carla worked with this woman on a specific presentation she would be presenting companywide; and when she gave it, rather than relying on a bullet-point PowerPoint presentation as many people do when they're not confident, she had a much more conversational and audience-focused style. She received tremendous affirmation and feedback from her boss and others.

What Carla teaches her clients, and what I have found as a speaker, is that like many other business and personal skills, speaking is something that improves with practice. The more you do it, the better you get, and therefore the less you fear it as your confidence grows.

## THE CHALLENGE: I NEED TO COMMUNICATE WITH INFLUENCE IN A MEMORABLE WAY

I don't recall when I officially decided I wanted to be a speaker, but my earliest visions looked like this: me on a big stage with spotlights and a headset microphone, a sea of people in a massive arena all on the edge of their seats furiously scribbling notes. I wasn't sure how any of this would transpire, but the thought stirred my heart and I knew it was something I wanted to pursue.

Moving toward this vision was a bit of an experimental process. Early in my career, I was not widely known as a speaker. I was simply the assistant alumni director at a private university, doing my best to be excellent and achieve the goals of the job.

One afternoon, my secretary mentioned that her church youth group in Glenpool, Oklahoma, was looking for a speaker for their weekly meeting. My first reaction was, *No thanks. That is not the size or type of group I have imagined.* My second reaction was, *Why not? I want to be a speaker, and this youth group is at least a start.* So I told her yes.

I put a lot of effort into preparing for that youth meeting. I spent time thinking about the kids who would attend and considered what I might tell them that would resonate and make a lasting impact on their lives.

I still remember the Thursday night I drove thirty miles outside of Tulsa to the meeting. About ten kids showed up that evening, a mix of ages and genders. I shared with them about the importance of having a vision for their lives and being committed to making a unique difference in the world. I spoke with passion and fervency, wanting nothing more than to inspire them to think big and go for their dreams.

Evidently my talk made an impact, because the youth leader called the next day to see if I would come back for the next four weeks and build on what I said in a series-type format. The following week the number of kids doubled, and every week going forward the attendance kept growing.

It wasn't a giant arena and I didn't need a microphone, but the experience confirmed that I was onto something.

As I progressed in my career, I kept accepting similar invitations to address small groups. Sometimes it was a handful of female leaders from the college campus who would gather in my living room. Other times it was speaking as a Junior League member to a group of media people and educators about a new curriculum that would benefit children in the community.

The more often I spoke publicly, the more comfortable and confident I became. Positive feedback spread, and before long I was speaking for larger groups both inside and outside my company. I kept honing my skills, and my speaking career grew.

Somewhere along the way, I began to recognize a pattern of preparation steps that I used repeatedly and still do. I believe they comprise a strategy for excellence in speaking that brings consistently positive results.

## THE STRATEGY: FOLLOW AN APPROACH TO SPEAKING THAT WORKS EVERY TIME

These few steps can work for you in virtually every situation that demands you to take the floor. It may be in your weekly staff meeting in front of a few familiar colleagues or in front of clients in a selling situation. These simple steps will help you become a speaker whom people want to listen to and will remember long after you finish.

### STEP #1: KNOW YOUR AUDIENCE

This first step is the most crucial one of all. Sonya Hamlin, author of *How to Talk So People Will Listen*, puts it this way: "It's all about focus. Whenever you start to talk, you first need to focus on your potential audience, whether it's one-on-one or a large group—and answer their basic question: 'What's in it for me if I listen to this?'"[4] Sonya's book is an excellent resource for anyone who speaks frequently or wants to make speaking a career.

> You must know what is on their minds and hearts so you can tailor your message to them and earn the right to keep them listening.

Can you remember the last time in formal events or informal office meetings that a speaker has really managed to capture your attention throughout their entire speech? Most speakers fail to give enough time to studying audience demographics or understanding what is really on their minds.

Before you address any audience, give considerable thought to who they are, what they care about, their worries, their questions, and their expectations in listening to you speak. You must know what is on their minds and hearts so you can tailor your message to them and earn the right to keep them listening.

In today's global marketplace, there are greater communication challenges than ever before. This is something the American Dairy Association discovered when they decided to take their highly successful "Got Milk?" campaign to Mexico and found out that the Spanish translation read, "Are you lactating?" The Coca-Cola name in China was first read as *Kekoukela,* meaning "Bite the wax tadpole" or "female horse stuffed with wax," depending on the dialect. Coke then researched forty thousand characters to find the phonetic equivalent *kokou kole,* which translated into "happiness in the mouth."[5] Global companies recognize the importance of these audience issues, and so must we.

There are actually two key people or people groups to know in any given speaking situation—the people you will actually address, and the person who has asked you to address them.

My first step in preparation is typically some research on the organization, usually via the Internet or interoffice resources if it is an internal group. Then I talk to the person who knows the most about the audience and the purpose of this particular session. Usually this is the person who has asked me to speak. I am committed not only to meet the needs of the audience but also to help the person in charge achieve his or her goals.

About a year ago, I was asked to give a keynote address for a women's networking organization based in northern New Jersey. I needed to understand the audience but also wanted to know what the president of the organization envisioned each person doing as a result of the event. As she and I talked, we explored the direction I could take and agreed that my speech should not only enhance their motivation for pursuing their own dreams but also ignite a greater commitment and affinity to the organization.

As we finished our discussion, I asked her, "At the end of my talk, what will it take to make you say, 'This was a huge success, and every dime I paid Lynette was more than worth it'?"

Her answer became my primary guide as I continued thinking about the women who would attend and planning my remarks. I connected one of my application tips to the mission of the organization, personally exhorting them to get more involved. The event received rave reviews from the attendees, and most importantly from the president, who was left with more invigorated, committed volunteers.

I also had a not-so-positive experience. I was invited by a large insurance agency to address a group of their agent office teams at a conference. The man organizing the event was extremely enthusiastic about my session, and we talked at length about the goals of the meeting and those who would attend.

As I began, it was clear that a rather disruptive table of women in the front were not interested in what I was saying. I plowed through my talking points, trying to focus on those who did seem to be enjoying it.

A few weeks later, I received a summary of the evaluations, and about one-third of the comments were completely opposite of my intentions, things like, "Lynette is so arrogant; we don't care at all about her big life or job in NYC." One woman gave me a minus ten below the lowest mark and added, "She was awful."

I tried to focus on the positive comments but couldn't get those stinging words out of my mind; they tormented me for days. In thinking back over the steps of preparation, I realized I could have been more diligent in understanding this audience and their unique priorities beyond what the organizer hd told me. The stories I shared must have seemed unrelated to the challenges of their daily lives, which were certainly quite different from those I faced in New York. Exhorting them to rise to a higher sense of calling in their work may have sounded superior and out of touch.

Instead of concluding that it was really their problem, I vowed to work even harder at connecting with my audiences and earning that trust from the moment I begin. My goal now is something summarized well by Jim Rohn, who has spoken to more than six thousand audiences worldwide. As he explains it, you don't want your audience to say, "So what?" but rather, "Me too!"

## STEP #2: PROVIDE AN OVERVIEW

Once you know as much as you can possibly know about your audience, begin your remarks by providing an overview. So much of the information we get these days comes in very small bites and is organized like segments of a TV newscast, stories in a newspaper, or listings from Internet searches.

Sonya Hamlin reminds us how much communication has changed:

- The attention span of the American public is now only 1½ minutes.
- People are in control of getting their own information, customizing, and editing to suit their exact needs.
- Time is a major issue. Succinct, clear, and to the point is today's imperative.

- We expect to get information super-fast and super-easily in small bites, highly organized and lean, with much variety and multimedia input.[6]

With these truths in mind, you will be much better received if you tell your audience what you are going to talk about up front and indicate what you hope they will take away. This helps them know how to listen and assists them in getting on track with you right from the start.

I have made this a regular practice in all settings where I'm speaking, whether a short presentation at work or lengthier sessions for large conferences. It is a courtesy to your listeners to let them know that you care about their time, you respect the investment they are making by listening, and you have something specific and tangible that you hope to give them as a return on their investment.

Let's say you are presenting to your division leadership team a new idea for a special event sales initiative. Rather than just getting up when it is your turn and beginning to talk, even if your topic is listed on the agenda, you instead start with the following.

Look around the room into as many eyes as possible and say, "You know from the agenda that I am going to address the proposed initiative for enhancing sales through 'innovative special events.' I am going to cover a few background points on what prompted this initiative, explain the critical success factors of launching it, and then propose a suggested timeline. I would welcome your interaction throughout the presentation but will also do a brief Q&A at the end. Our goal is to hear your feedback, then reach consensus on the concept before we finish today. If we are unable to reach that point, we will set another date for further discussion."

> It is a courtesy to your listeners to let them know that you care about their time, you respect the investment they are making by listening, and you have something specific and tangible that you hope to give them as a return on their investment.

What you have done in this brief, articulate introduction is made a promise. You have essentially said, "I care about your time and your ability to listen. Here is what I intend to accomplish and what you can expect to take away."

If you begin this way and then go on using the steps that follow here, you will be amazed at the effectiveness and impact you make each time you speak.

### STEP #3: ORGANIZE YOUR THOUGHTS AND SUMMARIZE

Arrange your thoughts into sections that you can title. This helps the audience listen more effectively and take notes if they like. It is similar to what chapters do for a book. They help you move through your reading and focus on one central theme for each bundle of pages.

When you move from section to section as you speak, you are building a rhythm for your listeners that helps them periodically take a breath and gather their thoughts about what you have just said.

> **As you finish a section, summarize the one key thought. If you can't summarize it, then you probably need to rethink your section.**

As you finish a section, summarize the one key thought. If you can't summarize it, then you probably need to rethink your section. What is it you are really trying to convey? Put it into one sentence as a title and then write another similar sentence that will summarize.

Have you ever known a speaker who has written out her entire talk and then read it to her audience? While this may provide a greater sense of security for the speaker, I find it to be a blatant form of disrespecting an audience. It makes me think, *If you are going to write it out word for word, then just e-mail it to me and let me read it at my convenience instead of watching the top of your head as you read it.* Imagine meeting someone for the first time and reading your greeting or introduction from an index card. Speaking is not all that different than reading, and with practice, you can learn how to speak effectively with only a few key notes to prompt you.

Sonya Hamlin recommends the following process for preparing speaking notes that I use as well:

> The biggest mistake people make when writing notes is that they write too much! Start with a good old outline form—your A, B, and C headings. Put in

two- or three-word descriptions to tell you what you'll be talking about. These are only catalysts to remind you about a talking point or section, not to spell it all out. You are so much more comfortable and effective as a speaker when each word is a trigger; you see the word and know what to talk about. Your bullets signify something you already know. For performance enhancement and continual eye contact, use the vertical process; look down, get the idea, look up to your audience and keep talking. Don't use the horizontal read-a-sentence method.[7]

## STEP #4: PERSONALIZE IT

Tell personal anecdotes that support the points you make. People connect to your message when they connect to you.

For instance, using the example of pitching a new sales initiative to my division leaders, I could tell them how the new initiative makes business sense, but let's say instead I

> **People connect to your message when they connect to you.**

paint the picture through words that describe the intended outcome, something like this: "Imagine that Hillary Howard from GE is going to attend the celebrity chef event, where she will be seated next to Bill Fisher, who is leading the GE account team. They will interact socially over the amazing filet mignon, and as a result Bill will schedule an appointment he has previously been unable to make."

The picture I just painted gave those leaders a personal look at what the event can do for sales. People have often told me several years after hearing one of my talks that what they remember is a story I told. Something about the story connected with them on a personal level.

Celina Realuyo, who is formerly the director for counterterrorism in the U.S. Department of State, works hard to personalize her high-level concepts.

I try to make what I do, even on a serious topic such as money laundering, very relevant to what is going on now for the audience. I often speak to school groups to explain how what we are doing to combat terrorism impacts them every day in their schools. It's a matter of relating these thirty-thousand-foot concepts to people's daily lives.

I also like to use comic relief that is real, natural, and relevant to their everyday experiences. Recently I was on my way to do a speech on enterprise risk man-

149

agement and pricing the risk of terrorism, when I had an accident in the taxi on the way and walked into the meeting with a huge bandage on my head. So I related it to the audience by saying, "Your chances of getting hit by a terrorist are much less than having an accident in a taxi."[8]

Don't be afraid to be vulnerable; share your struggles and how you worked through them. This is the best way to relate to your listeners, letting them know that you don't have all the answers but are on a very human journey as well. What sells at the newsstand—stories about the personal side of what people are going through—is what will help you connect with your listeners as well.

Bonnie St. John is an incredible speaker. A silver and bronze medalist in the 1984 Paralympics at Innsbruck, Austria, she also coaches executives, especially women of color, for key leadership posts. She and I were talking recently about how she prepares for her various speaking engagements.

When I go into a room and speak, I consider—why me, why them, why now? If you can't answer all those questions, then why bother? I want to make each speech a unique experience that brings us together for a reason. I think of my speaking as though I have a warehouse full of stories. I listen to what my client wants and then pull the right story. The way I tell that story depends on how they are listening. It's almost like cooking; you are preparing a meal that suits the occasion.

> **Not only are people looking for inspiration and instruction, but they also want to know what to do with it on Monday morning.**

Another thing I do is interview people from the organization where I'm going to speak. I don't just interview the senior leadership; I've learned I also need to talk to the rank and file. As a motivator, I need to listen to the leadership and where they want to go, then understand their people and why they're having trouble getting there. This is because personalizing is not just about me but also about them. Not only do I tell personal stories about myself, but the real way to be personal is to tell stories about them. Who they are right now and their issues—that is what's most important.[9]

### STEP #5: PROVIDE APPLICATION EXAMPLES

Not only are people looking for inspiration and instruction, but they also want to know what to do with it on Monday morning. Knowing they can take what you are saying and apply it is one more motivation for them to listen and remember what you say.

It is interesting to note that the average person remembers

10 percent of what they *read,*
26 percent of what they *hear,*
30 percent of what they *see,*
50 percent of what they *see and hear,*
70 percent of what they *say,* and
90 percent of what they *do.*[10]

Giving people tips on applying what they hear is going to give them a 90 percent chance of remembering what you say.

If I'm encouraging my audience to find good mentors and not wait until their boss gives them what they need, then I need to give at least a few tips on how they can do it. In this case, I make the point that we need strong mentors and then explain how to find them, approach them, and gain the input necessary for strong career growth.

Help your listeners take the inspiration and teaching you are offering and put it to work in their lives. If you are able to do this, they will listen more intently and feel a greater sense of personal benefit from what you've said.

An excellent speaker is something we can all become. We owe it to ourselves to work on our speaking skills, even if we don't plan to speak frequently in public ways.

Carla Kimball explains it like this:

> **Those who attempt to improve their ability to speak set themselves apart from the vast majority of the competition and crowd.**

Often people advance in their career because they are very good at the work, yet at a certain point it's no longer just the work that will move you forward. You have to be able to present yourself in staff meetings, with clients and the board. We are embarrassed to ask for this type of help, but we shouldn't be. Speaking with poise and confidence really can be learned, and I should know—I dropped out of every class in college that required me to speak in public because I was so afraid. And now thirty-five years later, I've taught literally hundreds of men and women how they can acquire the skills, be themselves, and present it well.[11]

Most fear it, few conquer it, but those who attempt to improve their ability to speak set themselves apart from the vast majority of the competition and crowd. To speak well, inside or outside our companies, is a learned ability that can advance our careers and gain us favor with others in ways that mere actions will not. One of my all-time favorite motivational speakers, Zig Ziglar, puts it this way: "You are the only person on earth who can use your ability."[12]

By stepping out and pushing our public speaking comfort zone to a new level, we will gain greater confidence and may even surprise ourselves with the excellent results.

*Mrs. Roosevelt was tall, gangly, with buckteeth, and had an odd squeaky voice, something we all found very funny. She sat us in a big circle, and as we drank our tea, she asked, "And what are you going to do to make a difference in this world?" Suddenly all the giggles stopped.*

—CAROLE HYATT
Founder and CEO,
The Leadership Forum

# NINE

# I Need Great Mentors, but Isn't Everyone Just Too Busy?

Think back one hundred years. Our great-grandmothers were working as hard as we do, either entirely at home or in home-related endeavors. And when they needed mentors, all they had to do was look across the spinning wheel to find a woman to be a role model, someone who could tell them the way life is supposed to go.

No need to describe how it is now; we all know it and live it. We may look around and see men and women who look like potential mentors sitting either next to us on the soccer field or down the hall in the larger cubicle. But everyone seems to be so busy that we are usually reluctant to ask or be asked. Still, most of us feel we need someone telling us if we're doing it right and hope we also have something of value to offer others.

## THE CHALLENGE: I NEED TO FIND
## AND RECRUIT MENTORS

Much has been written about mentoring. Tom Peters calls it the "Mentor Health System," and he suggests that mentoring is the best way to bring people along in this war for talent we hear so much about these days.[1]

Most everyone wants a mentor, yet many of us find it hard making the time to be one.

As I have talked to literally hundreds of female about this topic, interviewing many senior female executives while writing this book, I've found that mentoring is taking on many new dimensions and incorporates more now than it ever used to. While some of the old definitions remain, these days the concept of mentoring is far broader, which is great news for all of us.

> While some of the old definitions remain, these days the concept of mentoring is far broader, which is great news for all of us.

It is impossible in one chapter to cover the length and breadth of the topic of mentoring. Many excellent books, studies, and magazine articles have covered it well in the last several years. My goal here is simply to broaden your view of the mentors you have right now (many of whom you may not have noticed) and offer a few new ideas that can help you be sure that when it comes to mentoring, you are getting all you need and giving all you can amid the very busy life you lead.

Let's consider for a moment some new rules for mentoring.

| Traditional Rules | New Rules |
|---|---|
| Mentor chooses protégé. | Protégé chooses mentors. |
| It is an exclusive, privileged relationship. | You have many mentor/protégé relationships simultaneously. |
| Mentor invests in protégé. | Protégé has something to offer mentor in return. |

| Traditional Rules | New Rules |
|---|---|
| Mentor and protégé are similar and have much in common. | Mentor and protégé may be very different from each other; in fact, the contrast is often what makes the relationship work. |
| You are either a mentor *or* a protégé. | You are in the roles of both a mentor and a protégé, with different people, at different times. |
| The mentoring relationship is long-term. | The relationship is usually over a fixed period of time, typically a year or less. |

The contrast between the traditional and the new is not meant to imply that traditional is no longer relevant and new is better. The traditional rules produced great results and still do when implemented. The point here is that we should not be limited by traditional ways of thinking about mentoring. Our lifestyles have changed immensely, and we can all greatly benefit from a broader paradigm.

There are indeed many positives about the new rules of mentoring. Unlike the process of choosing teams in high school gym class, you don't have to wait to be selected. In fact, you shouldn't.

What you should do is think about where you want to go and the type of wisdom, input, and inspiration you need to get there more successfully and more enjoyably. Yes, *enjoyably.* That is worth something, isn't it? It can be lonely out there, and what a difference it makes to have a few people who sincerely care about where you are going and how you are succeeding in getting there.

What the new rules show us is that we are in a day of "empowered mentoring," mentoring that enables us to find for ourselves the people we want and need, and to do so in a way that fits our lifestyles.

Empowered mentoring demands that we do a number of things, including taking the initiative versus waiting for mentors to handpick us for themselves.

157

It also means that we may never actually meet all of our mentors face-to-face; we may simply read what they have written or hear them speak. We must be open to occasionally having only brief moments with our mentors.

## THE STRATEGY: EXPAND YOUR DEFINITION OF MENTORING

My primary mentor and dear friend Carole Hyatt has worked with women for more than thirty-five years as an international lecturer and best-selling author on career building. She has taught me a phrase that has helped frame my definition of mentoring—*mentoring moments.* This concept is something I believe is very well suited to the lifestyle we all live these days.

> **Rather than expect one or two individuals to meet one-on-one with us regularly, we should instead look for moments of exchange with people who offer nuggets of wisdom that we can apply.**

Carole believes, and I agree, that rather than expect one or two individuals to meet one-on-one with us regularly, we should instead look for moments of exchange with people who offer nuggets of wisdom that we can apply.

I have found this concept to work brilliantly in a variety of ways. Not only do I seek out these moments with a variety of people, but I also find I'm mentored via articles and books I read, by leaders I observe and admire from a distance, sometimes even through conversations I overhear in a bus or on the train. All of these sources briefly "mentor" me in ways I want and need for my personal life and career.

Carole had a mentoring moment when she was only eleven years old that she has never forgotten. She and a group of her young girlfriends were taking summer courses at a school located next door to the summer home of former first lady Eleanor Roosevelt. During the summers, Mrs. Roosevelt was in residence, so she would invite the young women of the school to come for tea. Carole explains,

## I Need Great Mentors, but Isn't Everyone Just Too Busy?

There were about twenty of us invited that day for tea. Mrs. Roosevelt was tall, gangly, with buckteeth, and had an odd squeaky voice, something we all found very funny. She sat us in a big circle, and as we drank our tea, she asked, "And what are you going to do to make a difference in this world?" Suddenly all the giggles stopped. We looked at her with amazement—no one had ever asked us that kind of question before. I had only been asked did I have my raincoat or what color of shoes was I going to wear?

As we sat there, for the first time we considered what our lives would be. When it was my turn, I said that I would like to have many children so I can be an influence in their lives. Now years later, while I only have one child of my own, my work has influenced literally thousands of people. That seed of an idea, of taking care of people and making an impact, began forming that day by the question asked by Mrs. Roosevelt. I call that a mentoring moment.[2]

Many of the women I have talked to mention these types of unexpected moments, times when we don't realize until later that we are being mentored. I think back to my first job as a placement counselor at a temporary help agency. I didn't realize then, and they probably didn't either, that those first three women I worked with so closely, my boss, Pat Davis, and two of the salespeople, Carol Wallace and Barbara Statuto, were my first mentors and role models in the corporate world. We did not sit down in a studious, focused way for a traditional mentoring relationship. Rather, we simply related day after day as we did our jobs. I was full of questions and they provided answers, not always verbally but often in what they modeled and how they worked.

If you desire to be mentored or to mentor others but you lack big blocks of time, try adjusting your definition and looking for creative ways to recognize and partake of mentoring moments.

**If you desire to be mentored or to mentor others but you lack big blocks of time, try adjusting your definition and looking for creative ways to recognize and partake of mentoring moments.**

Last summer while my husband, Ron, and I were traveling with our boys in Africa, I was introduced to a woman running for president in one of the nations we were visiting. She shared about her vision and the obstacles she would need to overcome in order to win the election. I offered to continue dialoguing in coming months about ideas and solutions to assist her further. She was so encouraged by our first conversation, a mentoring moment, that she called the next day to ask if she could fly to meet us again in another nation we'd be visiting. So ten days later, we were together again, this time including several other experts I had invited to join the discussion to offer her additional ideas and help. She and I have continued our conversations over the last year and now consider each other friends.

Regardless of how your empowered mentoring occurs, there are three definitive stages that, if you understand and follow them, will help you succeed in the area of mentoring. Each stage has a joy of its own and can afford unique mentoring benefits that are certainly worth the effort.

## STAGE #1: IDENTIFY YOUR MENTORS

Pinpointing your mentors can be a fun and motivating stage for getting your creative juices flowing. Just the process of considering who you want to learn from is a stimulating exercise.

Two filters to use in identifying your potential mentors are these:

1. Who do I admire?
2. Who do I need?

I like to start with "Who do I admire?" because is it is the most exhilarating way to begin a mentoring relationship. Take a few moments to think outside your own box of possibility and consider this question: if you could learn from anyone, who would it be?

You first will need to believe the fact, and it is a fact, that everyone is accessible—*everyone*. You've perhaps heard of the "six degrees of separation." The fact is that you are actually more like three degrees (people) away from anyone in the world you need to know.

When I say this in networking workshops I'm conducting, the first reaction may be like the one you just had—a skeptical chuckle. I will then ask someone to name a person they want to know whom they consider a long shot. Typically someone names a world leader such as Condoleezza Rice or a celebrity such as Oprah Winfrey.

### I Need Great Mentors, but Isn't Everyone Just Too Busy?

Without exception, someone in the room of typically twenty people is either one or two steps from the person mentioned, every time. I have tried this experiment over and over, sometimes with a bit of trepidation wondering if it will again hold true, and it always does, even in the most random, seemingly noninfluential groups of people.

What this shows is that everyone in the world is indeed accessible. If that's true, then what keeps us from believing in the potential of reaching anyone we want or need to reach at any time?

It is quite often our own internal sense of inadequacy. We tend to feel somewhat undeserving of someone's time, especially if they are a high-profile person. We feel awkward and unsure of how we would approach them and warrant their attention.

I was watching a fascinating interview the other night on TV that supports this reality. Larry King was interviewing Donald Trump. What struck me most about Mr. Trump is how open and interested he is in new ideas, all the time. When he mentioned several of his latest ventures, King asked him how he got these ideas. Trump responded, "Smart people come to me with the idea; it sounds great and presents significant potential, so I go for it."[3]

When I heard him say this, I was intrigued that despite of the level of fame and fortune he enjoys, Donald Trump is still accessible when the right people come to him with the right ideas.

### CLOSER THAN WE THINK

I learned this myself in writing this book. I knew I wanted to interview some top female leaders, but I also knew that they are extremely busy and that many would have no idea who I am or whether or not this book was worth their time.

I started the process the way I'm telling you to start, by identifying the women I really admired and wanted to interview, along with those whom I felt the book needed. I then used my networks of people, one or two removed, to approach them. I was surprised and delighted that virtually every single person said yes. And you and I are the beneficiaries of their wisdom.

I learned years ago while organizing many fund-raising events that people often say yes to something not so much because of *what* it is but because of *who* is asking. This is true for all of us in a busy, hectic world. We sift through snail mail, e-mails, and phone messages, prioritizing them most often by who sent each one and our perception of personal gain in answering them.

Put this reality to work for you. Once you have narrowed down your list of the people you want to know, start looking for people they already know whom you also know or could know.

As you think about whom you would *like* to know and be mentored by in some way, think next about whom you *need.*

This is a great time to go back to your purpose statement, your personal brand plan, or your board of directors. Think about who you need to help you get to the next place of success in your key area of focus, be that training, development, branding, encouragement, work/life balance, or some other area.

Unlike your personal board members, whom you look to for assistance on a project-by-project basis, your mentors are people who will likely invest in the overall picture of your life. It may be that a board member is also a mentor, but the focus in mentoring is the total of your career or life. Your personal board members, on the other hand, are those you will call on for a very specific talent or expertise related to a project, such as investing in a start-up company, learning a new skill at work, an introduction they can make for you, and so forth.

So consider what needs for advice and instruction you have in your life and career right now, and determine who might be the best mentor in helping you meet those needs. Again, think outside your box and aspire to be mentored by the best of the best in the areas of your need.

## STAGE #2: ASK YOUR MENTORS

As I mentioned, mentoring may not always occur face-to-face. When you are choosing mentors from a distance, you may not even have to ask them to be mentors at all, as is the case when you're reading a powerful book or article.

But on those occasions when asking is essential in order to request a person's time, there are some simple, practical, yet often overlooked ways to ask in a way that will increase your chances of receiving a yes.

*Start with the principle of serving.* Regardless of how popular, famous, or busy someone is, everyone has needs or things they would like to have or do. If you can offer something someone needs or wants, you are more likely to gain their mentoring in return.

Recently a young woman whom I did not know wrote me an e-mail indicating her interest in spending time together, hoping I might consider mentoring her. I replied to her e-mail, indicating that while I was honored by her interest,

I was currently involved in several new projects that left no time for adding a new mentee. I thanked her for her interest and encouraged her not to give up the search for a mentor.

Her response got my attention and struck a significant chord of interest. Instead of responding to my e-mail by saying, "Thank you, I understand," she instead said, "Lynette, I so appreciate how busy you are. I would be glad to just run errands for you, do your laundry, anything that would be helpful in serving your life and vision right now." Wow, she had touched on some legitimate needs I had. And her willingness to serve in these ways made me realize I would be sorry to pass her by.

Then, before I responded to that e-mail, she wrote me again, telling me how excited she was about the book I was writing and its potential to impact women's lives. She had even polled some of the women at her ad agency to get their creative ideas about promoting my book.

What she had done was serve my need and touch my heart. I suddenly wanted her life-giving spirit around me, and I knew I could find a way to make any time spent together a benefit to both of us.

It's been months since then, and she has become one of my most trusted supporters and friends in the journey of writing this book. She has offered tangible help from the beginning through her creative talents and encouraging words. I, in turn, have helped her sort out her dreams and find hope in this stage of her career. It's been a win-win relationship for both of us.

When you are asking someone to be your mentor, consider what you can offer them as part of a win-win relationship. Do some research ahead of time to find out what they have done, what they are currently doing, and what might best serve their current interests or needs.

> When you are asking someone to be your mentor, consider what you can offer her as part of a win-win relationship.

*Ask and answer the questions "Why?" and "What?"* After you have answered the questions "Who do I admire?" and "Who do I need?" you will want to go back to that all-important question: Why? Why do you want or need the person to mentor you? It is an important question to answer, because it will help you in the initial stage of asking. Knowing why you are seeking that person for a mentoring relationship also helps you measure later the impact the person has made, something you will need for the third stage of acknowledging.

To give you an example, here is how it went for me with my mentor Carole Hyatt about four years ago. I met Carole for the first time at her home when I attended one of her Leadership Forum "Getting to Next" workshops in January 1990. I absolutely loved the two-day workshop and was introduced to some of the most accomplished and exciting women I had met thus far in my career.

As I walked out the door of her home that day, Carole looked me in the eye and said, "If I can ever be of help to you, please let me know." By this time in my career, I had heard similar sentiments expressed many times, often in order to be polite but seldom in a sincere way. I could tell Carole meant it, and I spent the next week thinking about how I could best respond to her generous offer.

It was clear that Carole was a much-in-demand speaker, author, educator, and friend to hundreds across the globe. If I was going to ask for any of her time, I had to be clear on exactly why I needed it. I also had to determine what I might offer her in return.

I dropped her a thank-you note and indicated I would be calling her. In the meantime, I became certain about why I needed her as a mentor. *I want to know Carole Hyatt because she can help me get better connected to successful women in New York City, and she can help prioritize my special interests that are outside my current job description and projects I'd like to actively pursue.*

I now knew *why*, but I also needed to know *what*. What exactly was I going to ask her for? I determined that I would ask her for a brief time to talk about an upcoming major speaking engagement, one I had been preparing for and planning toward for months.

I made the phone call, we set up a time to meet, and a few weeks later I was walking with Carole around the reservoir in Central Park on a brisk February morning. This was just a few weeks before my major event. As we walked, Carole asked about my goals for this event and offered very practical tips on how I could leverage it to open further doors for speaking and writing.

As we were rounding the last bend in our walk, she asked, "Why don't you come to the next Leadership Forum workshop, Lynette, and test your material by speaking to our attendees?"

It was a tremendous offer, and I jumped on it. Just one week later, I spoke to the group. A day or so after, Carole and I were on the phone talking about simple yet powerful ways I could improve my presentation even further.

After the event, at Carole's invitation, we met again for a debriefing on how it went, and then every several months thereafter we would get together to talk about how I was progressing or to discuss some of her new ventures and how I might be involved.

This mentoring relationship, more than any others in my career, has been a powerful, encouraging gift in so many ways. Neither of us knew at the beginning where it would go, what we would offer to each other, how often we would meet, or how our relationship would evolve. But we dove in and both reaped some great rewards.

Carole shared with me recently her perspective on how our relationship began.

> You had a very clear vision of where you wanted to go, you were extremely focused, and you sent the best thank-you note I've ever received. I have a strong need to mentor for inner satisfaction, and you appealed to that need. You were also very generous, not just a taker but eager to give back wherever you could. I liked your ideas and being able to contribute to them. It is an honor to have someone like you in my life, someone younger with great energy and focus.[4]

We both agree that in the last year or two we have moved beyond mentor and protégé to becoming true friends and business partners. Ron and I have spent time with Carole and her husband, Gordon, including a weekend last summer in their beautiful home in the Berkshires. She and I are now involved in a joint business venture combining our expertise into a workshop that builds business relationships between executive women from major corporations.

All of this because I figured out in the beginning why I was approaching her and specifically what I needed when I asked.

In the book *Learning from Other Women*, Carolyn S. Duff summarizes some further ways to initiate a mentor relationship with a woman who may be in a far superior job or station in life.

> You prepare. You learn about this woman you admire and most likely wish to emulate. Where has she been? What has she accomplished? You develop a list of what you want to learn, your goals and your expectations. Very important, you

consider what you can contribute to a reciprocal relationship—how you can provide support for her goals. Then you approach her with respect for her available time and her image/visibility. You say what you admire and how you see that she could help you develop. You do not demand. You prepare.[5]

## STAGE #3: ACKNOWLEDGE YOUR MENTORS

In chapter 6, we looked at specific ways to acknowledge your personal board members. The same principles hold true for mentors. A key to effective acknowledgment is always considering what means the most to the person whom you want to thank.

With time being such a precious commodity in our lives, anyone who shares their time with you, even your colleagues or those who work for you, deserves a thank-you—if not in a formal manner, then certainly with a sincere look in the eye and a smile.

> Anyone who shares their time with you, even your colleagues or those who work for you, deserves a thank-you.

Practicing this attitude of gratitude has many benefits beyond blessing the recipient. For starters, it cultivates a heart of gratefulness and gives you a greater sense of meaning and joy. The more often I say thanks, the more thankful I become.

As I was putting the finishing touches on this book, I received a surprise acknowledgment that moved my heart deeply. A woman left a shopping bag and a handwritten card with my name on it by Ron's chair at a church service one Sunday night in New York. I was in our home in Raleigh, having just sent my final manuscript to the editor, when Ron mentioned to me on the phone that he had this gift there waiting for me. "Open it!" I said. He proceeded to read the card.

The words were deeply encouraging. The woman mentioned how she appreciated my mentoring from a distance and the role model she found me to be. It was one of the most eloquent, poignant cards I have received in a long time. Then my husband opened the gift. It was an incredible Chanel handbag. I was thrilled and humbled at the same time. This dear woman had no idea that for two years I would wander into the Chanel sections of Bloomingdale's or Saks Fifth Avenue, admiring the beautiful bags but not feeling the liberty to buy one for myself.

Her lavish gift and the beautiful card came at the perfect moment, after months of exhaustion and sacrifices writing this book. I sat there weeping, amazed at her generosity, grateful for the privilege of being a mentor at least for one wonderful woman.

## MORE CREATIVE IDEAS FOR MENTORING

Outside of personal, one-on-one interactions, here are a few favorite mentoring ideas gleaned from my own experience and that of many women I know.

*Books.* Never discount the impact of mentoring received via books. I once read an article that I absolutely loved by Charlie "Tremendous" Jones, a well-known speaker. Charlie writes,

> A few simple changes in your daily routine can improve the quality of your life. From now on when you read a book, make the author your mentor and always read with your pen in your hand. As you get used to reading with a pen in hand, you begin to cultivate the habit of making notes of things you actually think, in addition to what you thought you read. We must learn to read, but only to get our own minds in motion and start our thought processes.[6]

Denise Johnston, president of the adult division at The Gap, told me how she is mentored while driving from Manhattan out to her home in the Hamptons each weekend.

> I listen to all of the bestselling books on tape, and as I do, everything starts coming together in my mind. These authors are sharing what they did and how they learned, and it's amazing how great the timing will be for what I'm going through in business. Sometimes it's about strategy, leadership, organizational restructuring, or the process of having a great idea come to light. They all share how it happened for them, and when I listen, I am able to translate their learnings for myself.[7]

*Peers.* During the two days I spent attending Carole Hyatt's "Getting to Next" workshop, there were six of us who really sensed a connection and chemistry with one another. So we decided to meet again the following month to continue the process of presenting offers and requests related to moving our dreams and ideas forward.

What began as a one-time follow-up lunch became a monthly mentoring moment for all of us throughout the next two years. We rotated among one another's homes or offices, and we took turns receiving mentoring input and counsel about our challenges or ideas at the time. Over those two years, we launched new businesses, quit jobs, changed companies, and were absolutely invigorated with the valuable relationships we discovered in one another.

We were talking recently about why our group worked so well. Our conclusions included the following:

- *Mutual respect and admiration.* "I was so honored to be included in this group of achieved women I admired so greatly."
- *Emotional support.* "Having all that experience to query along with getting feedback, advice, and points of view was emotionally and intellectually stimulating. That sense of community where I thought there was none was such a wonderful thing."
- *Transparent honesty.* "What a privilege to have women at the top of their game all speaking from the benefit of their professional experiences, saying, 'Did you think about this?' or 'What about that?' Holding off your own reaction to let in other ideas is so crucial. We do that in business under 'creative brainstorming,' and now we were doing it for one another."

> Peer mentoring groups can be powerful. If you can't find one, start one and watch how much difference even occasional gatherings can make.

Peer mentoring groups can be powerful. If you can't find one, start one and watch how much difference even occasional gatherings can make.

Individual peers can also be terrific mentors. Cathy Benko, leader of Deloitte's National Women's Initiative, shared with me this same philosophy that emerged from her personal experiences.

I don't believe mentoring has to be or should be with a person of "position." I've had many different, phenomenal relationships with people up, down, and sideways on the

168

corporate ladder, men and women who have gone out of their way to support me in some way. I didn't label them mentors at the time, never thought of the term. It has always been a very natural thing—not contrived. I never thought, *Let me go find the president of the company and ask him or her to be my mentor,* but rather they come from very simple, practical places. Most people look right at the top and forget everyone in between.[8]

Joyce Roche, president of Girls Inc., agrees:

A mentor isn't necessarily someone high up in the company. A mentor can be on your same level or just one step ahead. It is great to have a mentor who may be the senior leader, someone who understands and guides you and can drop your name in favorable ways, saying, "Let's keep our eye on her," but you never know when that person just one step ahead of you may be in a meeting and can also say, "She's done great things, and we should give her a shot." I've even had some great mentors who reported to me. They've pulled my coattails and said, "Here's what I'm hearing and how you're being perceived." They're not doing it viciously; they believe in me and want to be sure I have what I need to know.[9]

*Lectures.* Similar to reading books, listening to speakers you admire can be almost as good as inviting them out to lunch. If you buy their tapes or DVDs, you can even repeat the impartation over and over again. When you find speakers you connect with or admire, visit their Web sites, subscribe to their newsletters, respond to their blogs, and go to hear them speak whenever you can. Whether or not you meet them personally, you will still have access to all of their best lessons and ideas, with little cost or investment other than your time.

> You probably already are a mentor to more people than you realize.

Now is definitely your moment for mentoring. Make the mentoring relationship what you need it to be. Keep with the traditional rules if they work, but be open to defining it as so much more. Recognize the myriad mentors you already have within reach.

As far as being a mentor to others, you probably already are a mentor to more people than you realize. Instead of feeling guilty that you aren't taking them to lunch and plowing deep into their hearts, just continue making the most of every interaction, even on the fly.

A Spanish proverb I like so much says it well: "More grows in the garden than the gardener knows he has sown." Mentoring is one of the great ways we garden. Only over time will we recognize all the significant people and lives we have grown and the gardens in which we have blossomed.

*Those were hard times, and I was absolutely exhausted. I was executive platinum on American Airlines, many times waking up in the morning not knowing what city or country I was in, yet it was a tremendous, life-changing experience, reinforcing what we all know but I got to experience on a day-to-day basis—that human beings everywhere basically want the same thing. We want to know who we can count on.*

—DIANA INGRAM
Director for Emerging
Business Opportunities, IBM

# TEN

# Different Than What I Thought, Better Than What I Imagined

Let's recount where we've been for a moment. In this journey of employing new, practical tools in your life and work, you have written a purpose statement that brings deeper direction and meaning. You are striving toward personal wholeness and becoming an agent of wholeness in your workplace. You have organized a personal board, put together a personal brand plan, are becoming a better communicator, and have identified a wide variety of mentors you need.

So now what? No matter how hard you work or how dedicated you are, you will be surprised. Surprised at how different the journey will be than you thought when you were just starting out. Surprised at the struggles and seemingly endless periods of waiting that will come. Disappointed in the relationships that didn't work out like you hoped, or promises that were broken, or advantages taken when you tried so hard to be wise and strong.

Fortunately, it's the unplanned surprises that can be the real gifts in the end. I was talking to Diana Ingram, director for emerging business opportunities at IBM, and we were reflecting on the surprise twists and turns our careers have taken. I loved this story she shared with me, and I think it will encourage you as well.

The toughest assignment I ever had was when I was VP of the communications sector in Latin America, based in Miami. When I got there, I found a demoralized team that had not achieved their goals in three years. So here I was, responsible for twenty-something countries. It was like changing the tires on an Indy car in the middle of a race.

Two of the general managers, both Latin-American men, were being "reorganized out," and I was put in their place. One of them had gone behind my back to some of his former direct reports, saying, "She probably got here by sleeping around." I in turn said to the person who shared this gossip, "Do you think the IBM Corporation would really turn over a $400 million entity to someone unqualified who got ahead like that?"

Needless to say, those were very challenging times. When I was offered the assignment, the first person I called was my mom, who was very enthusiastic about the new opportunity and said, "You are going to do the very best you can in every moment, and that's all you can ask. It's going to be great." She was right; I didn't know what to do, but I was determined I was going to do it.

It was heavy lifting every step of the way, for two years, eight quarters. At our first major meeting, a few of my new team members were saying, "This is so hard; the U.S. doesn't understand how it is in Latin America," to which I replied, "Here's the deal: Rule number one, we make our numbers. We are making $400 million for the IBM Corporation this year. This part is not up for discussion. What is up for discussion is how we do it. So let's spend our time figuring out how we will do it. If you, gentlemen, are afraid to escalate, then let me know, because I for one am not afraid to do it."

This team who had failed to make their numbers, made the numbers seven out of eight quarters and for both of the years we were together. We rolled up our sleeves, got rid of the rocks in our hands, set performance expectations, and helped one another go after them.

Those were hard times, and I was absolutely exhausted. I was executive platinum on American Airlines, many times waking up in the morning not knowing what city or country I was in, yet it was a tremendous, life-changing experience, reinforcing what we all know but I got to experience on a day-to-day basis—that human beings everywhere basically want the same thing. We want to know who we can count on.

I count those great people as my friends now. I admire and respect what they do and what they did. After a team dinner following the start of our second year together, one of my team members came to me and said, "We are with *you*." We adapted to one another, and it was a very, very special time.[1]

Tough times, exhaustion, unplanned twists and turns . . . All of these can be surprise gifts. Such is the journey for each of us along the path and up the ladder of what we call our careers.

> You and I are on a pathway toward greatness—great not because we craft it perfectly but because we embrace fully every surprise that comes.

You and I are on a pathway toward greatness—great not because we craft it perfectly but because we embrace fully every surprise that comes.

## THE CHALLENGE: MY JOURNEY DOESN'T LOOK LIKE I THOUGHT IT WOULD

I particularly enjoy speaking to college graduates in their early twenties. They have finished their undergraduate degrees and are excited about the future, yet they often feel intimidated by the daunting task of finding that first job or knowing how to begin on the pathway toward their dreams.

I often share with them about preparing for greatness, explaining what it will take to get from where they are now to where they want to be. The first thing I tell them is, "It will look different than what you are thinking but will be better than what you expect. Be ready for the unexpected. Accept surprises. Look for new ways of working with what you have been given. Become an artist who designs your own life out of surprise elements."

Artists have a way of taking simple, even ugly elements and turning them into something of beauty. The block of marble from which Michelangelo carved his famous sculpture of David had been already hacked on by two other artists, Agostino di Duccio and Antonio Rossellino. It is said they attempted to carve from it but abandoned their projects because of a lack of experience and skill. I would also add a lack of ambition and vision to this list.

The marble was neglected and exposed to the elements for twenty-five years before Michelangelo, at the age of twenty-six, was commissioned to do the work. The result after three years of labor was a masterpiece inspiring awe in millions since 1504.

There are so many others we hear of who have taken their surprises—sometimes seen as challenges—and fashioned something beautiful from them.

I have been a fan of Martha Stewart since her early days, subscribing to her magazine from the first issue and watching her television programs over the years. Certainly Martha did not envision a prison term as part of her journey. Still, in her characteristic unrelenting style, she faced her sentence with a determination not to give in to the pressure and quit.

In her book *Martha Rules*, she describes her time in prison.

> There were many things I had missed—my animals, my homes, fresh food, travel, and the daily challenges of managing an endlessly interesting business. But there were just as many wonderful things that I had gathered during those 5 months—new friendships, so many ideas, and so much information and knowledge from fascinating books that I actually had the time to read. I also gained a new appreciation for the complexity of every single person's situation.[2]

One of my best friends is going through a tough time with her mother, who has Alzheimer's. At eighty-six years old, her mom is experiencing memory loss and increasing dependency on others for help with even the simplest life tasks. Kathi, an achieved professional who left the corporate world a few years ago to pursue her own design business, has struggled with this surprise twist in her road. In a recent e-mail, she described it like this:

> I've got to admit, it's been a difficult winter for me and I've wondered a few times if I'm going to be able to persevere through this time with my mom. It feels quite lonely, to be honest. But just over the last couple of months, God has brought a couple of people into my life who have gone or are currently going through a similar situation, so I am feeling more supported than I have in quite some time.[3]

At times like these, and there will be many, we must remember that surprises are almost always gifts. Life is full of them, so many to be grateful for and so much to celebrate.

The sound of birds chirping is such a sweet thing. I hear them on early morning runs when the world is still waking up. They could have been created as just small, insignificant creatures without voices, and yet they sing. Flowers, beautiful in themselves, include the gift of fragrance.

> **Although things go differently than we think they will, so often in the end they turn out better than we expected.**

Gifts are everywhere and simply require eyes that are willing and eager to see. Remembering this has helped me in my journey as I have grown to accept that in spite of my plans and my commitment to being organized and in charge, I simply cannot control much of what life brings. One of the gifts of growing older is that we have increasingly more personal experiences to validate the fact that although things go differently than we think they will, so often in the end they turn out better than we expected.

## THE STRATEGY: VIEW YOUR LIFE THROUGH THE LENS OF HOPE AND POSSIBILITY

We began in chapter 1 by talking about the benefits of knowing and defining our purpose, the answer to the question, "why?" Purpose helps us see and discover life's gifts through our own unique lens, bringing personal meaning to the seemingly random things that happen to us and through us.

There are some unique principles about purpose that I believe summarize much of what we have been learning throughout this book. Each one has brought me tremendous strength along the journey, especially when things don't look quite like I thought they would.

### PRINCIPLE #1: POWER

We often attribute power to a position, a paycheck, or popularity. But consider someone powerful who has no title at all, someone like Mother Teresa, a woman with tremendous influence, a winner of the Congressional Medal of Honor and the Nobel Peace Prize, among countless other recognitions and awards.

This precious woman had no title, no large paycheck, and no corner office. Yet she was powerful because she understood her purpose. "I feel called to help individuals, to love each human being," she said. "I never think in terms of crowds in general but in terms of persons. Were I to think about crowds, I would never begin anything. It is the person that matters. I believe in person-to-person encounters."[4]

Often we look at our job descriptions or circumstances and conclude that we are powerless. So we choose just to keep on working, unfulfilled and unstimulated.

It was this tremendous frustration in my own life that propelled me toward answering the overriding *why* question. As I answered the question by determining my purpose (to inspire and motivate people), I sensed a new level of power in my life. More and more people have been drawn to my ideas both at work and in my personal pursuits, even though circumstances often have not changed at all.

> **Purpose gives you power that no one can give or take from you.**

Purpose gives you power that no one can give or take from you. If you don't like the word *power*, then think *em*power, something most women naturally seek to do for themselves and others. Purpose empowers you. It is your most important gift; it puts you on the pathway to greatness and gives you deep, lasting meaning each step of the way.

### PRINCIPLE #2: UNIQUENESS

All of us on some level are part of a corporate purpose, whether in our work, in our families, or in groups we serve. But within those corporate purposes is a purpose unique to you, a contribution only you can make.

Viktor Frankl believed, "Everyone has their own specific vocation or mission in life. . . . Therein, we cannot be replaced, nor can our lives be repeated. Thus, everyone's task is as unique as their specific opportunity to implement it."[5]

When I was working in a senior marketing role at Deloitte, there were many who shared the same job title. Yet among us were a vast array of personalities, experiences, ways of approaching marketing, and preferences for certain tasks and activities. We were each very unique despite the fact we shared the same job description.

When I first moved to New York, it was hard not to be intimidated by their talent and experience. Here I was coming from Tulsa, Oklahoma, with no Ivy League college degree or background on Wall Street. I was uncertain about my ability to measure up.

Fortunately, I spent a great deal of time assessing exactly why I was moving to NYC in the first place, leaving a fifteen-year career in a city where I was known and had already found my place in many leadership roles. Understanding why this job at this time was right, and why I could make a unique contribution, helped me make it through those early days of intimidation. I spent more time focused on making a significant contribution and less time worrying about whether or not I measured up or stood out from the others.

> **Don't miss the uniqueness of your life and your story; it is a gift.**

Your purpose articulates why you are unique and explains what differentiates you. Understanding this eliminates the sense of competition that can so easily pervade teams. Your purpose helps you explain to yourself and to others why you are uniquely qualified and have an important role to play.

Your journey right now is earning you unique credibility to be an expert and authority on something. Don't miss the uniqueness of your life and your story; it is a gift.

## PRINCIPLE #3: RESULTS

The typical definition of *purpose* includes the word *intention*. Intention implies an end result, an intended outcome.

We are a results-oriented culture, enamored with those who achieve goals and make their marks. This orientation, however, can be a problem when you're in a season that isn't giving you the results you thought you'd be getting. Maybe the promotion didn't come through, or the raise was nothing like you thought it would be. How do you get through those times without growing bitter?

This is one of the times (and there are so many) when purpose helps us see the same scenario with a new view. Purpose helps us measure results differently.

I shared in chapter 1 about the day when a frustrating commute triggered great discouragement, and I sat crying at my desk. This was when understanding my purpose on a broader level became such a gift. I considered the handful of people in my circles of influence, including Sandra in the office next door, and could recognize the impact I'd been having on their lives. I could see that my personal purpose "to inspire and motivate others to live lives of hope, overcoming every challenge on the way to their dreams" was indeed happening. It helped me see results that were not visible via the usual avenues that we want so much to reward us.

## PRINCIPLE #4: PROTECTION

Have you ever had a job that wasn't right for you or people in your life who pulled you down? Purpose will protect you from making wrong choices.

Many a bad partnership could have been avoided if only the individuals had asked each other, "Why?" Why are we building this company? Why should we spend our lives together? Why do you do what you do?"

> Defining our purpose
> helps us become good
> stewards of
> ourselves—our time,
> talents, and
> treasures. Only we
> can guard and
> protect these most
> precious gifts.

I was a single woman until two years ago, and many of my well-intentioned friends were eager to help me find Mr. Right. This meant a host of blind dates over a period of twenty years, dates totaling roughly sixty-five (I counted one day out of exasperated curiosity!)

Over the course of time, I became quite good at the usual process. It would typically go something like this:

"Lynette, would you be open to meeting someone I have in mind?" In my early years, I would say, "Sure, I like to be open to any and all possibilities. Who knows when things might just click?"

Then after the date, I'd dramatically chide to my sister or mom, "What were they thinking? This guy could not be any less my type than if I'd ran a personal ad describing someone else."

And so it went for many years.

Then I got in tune with my purpose, defining associated aspirations and goals. Now, instead, the scenario would go something like this:

"Lynette, would you be open to meeting someone I have in mind?"

"Well, possibly. Tell me more about him. Where is he going in life? What does he want to do and why? How would he feel about a woman who wants to inspire and motivate people by being a writer and speaker? Would this intimidate or attract him?"

Most of the time this is where the conversation ended. Though I would have a tinge of disappointment, I was grateful that I'd avoided frustration over spending precious time with someone who had no real benefit for my present or my future.

This isn't meant to sound elitist or arrogant. Many of the guys I said no to were great men. I am simply proposing that defining our purpose helps us become good stewards of our time, talents, and treasure. Only we can guard and protect these most precious gifts.

A well-defined purpose is your filter, protecting you from the wrong people, the wrong job, discouragement when desired results tarry, and time wasted on even good things that end up being enemies of the best.

## PRINCIPLE #5: OTHERS

Your purpose, if it is going to fully ignite your heart and soul, must somehow include a dimension of service to others.

I said before that greatness is not about the approval or applause of the masses. Our purpose, though, must somehow connect to serving others if lasting fulfillment is what we are after.

As you consider your purpose, think about how you intend to impact others. Your purpose statement and, more important, your life should tell anyone who hears it or is watching it what a difference you are making in people's lives. Having a purpose statement that includes others helps you measure your results differently—not by your paycheck, title, or the recognition of others, though those things will come, but rather by the difference you are making for people.

> Impacting others is the most important aspect of your purpose and the key to bringing lasting joy and fulfillment in life.

Impacting others is the most important aspect of your purpose and the key to bringing lasting joy and fulfillment in life. Our motivation and satisfaction are ignited by knowing that what we do is not only for our own benefit but for the benefit of others.

People who know and live their purpose make a powerful impact on others every step of the way.

## PRINCIPLE #6: SATISFACTION

As a person who knows and understands your purpose, you will experience deep and lasting satisfaction. Regardless of the hurdles you face, the money you are not yet making, the things you're still waiting for, and the resistance that may come your way, you can be deeply, richly satisfied as you do what you know you are made to do. You may be sweeping floors or waiting tables, but if doing so aligns with your purpose, you can go home satisfied, knowing you are making a unique difference in the world.

Satisfaction could possibly be one of the most sought-after yet elusive things in the workplace. According to a poll taken by CareerWomen.com, nearly half of the women polled said they are staying in jobs that are not satisfying. They say that to be satisfied, they want to feel respected, to be of service, and to be challenged in their careers. Jillian Donnelly of CareerWomen.com says companies are at a real risk of losing talented employees for lack of satisfaction. "What we found most interesting in this survey is that women are not primarily inspired by compensation, but by respect, service, and challenge. Job seekers are clearly looking for challenging work, but in an environment where they 'fit.'"[6]

On many levels, satisfaction is a choice. We decide to be satisfied right now, in the place we find ourselves today.

In my years of singleness, probably sometime in my later thirties, I decided, "Hey, life is now, not someday when I get married. I don't want to miss out on the gifts coming my way just because the thing I want most isn't happening." So I simply chose to be satisfied.

I searched for ways to more creatively live my purpose in my job and personal pursuits, and as a result my satisfaction grew. Of course, there were still times when my longing to be married seemed like the biggest, most overwhelming issue in my life, but knowing that I was pursuing my dreams in ways in which I was empowered helped my satisfaction and thus my contentment grow.

Now that I am married to the husband of my dreams, I am even more grateful that I chose to be personally satisfied before I met and married Ron. If I had not, I think I would be a bit disappointed in marriage. Why? Because marriage cannot ever satisfy me entirely. I am created to live a life of purpose, and when I am doing that, I am satisfied—in my marriage, my work, and even the challenges I face day to day.

So many women are unsatisfied, and they have bought into the lie of our culture that their dissatisfaction in life is the result of not having a perfect relationship. Having now lived both with a marriage relationship and without one, I know with great certainty that the relationship is not the end-all goal. My marriage enhances my levels of joy and satisfaction, but it does not, and cannot, guarantee them.

My friend Debora Grobman was married at nineteen and explains an epiphany moment that took her to a new place of satisfaction.

I was living in Westchester, New York, in the mid-seventies, with my husband and four little girls ages six to thirteen. My life was about carpooling and being a mom. One day I was driving after school with twelve kids in my station wagon. Suddenly I realized there were tears streaming down my face and not one of the kids noticed I was crying. Could it be that who the driver was didn't really matter?

I thought a lot about it alone that night after everyone was asleep. I realized that I needed something more to challenge my brain. This led me on a mission to find out what it was that I really wanted to do. I chose to go to law school. I thought about going at nights but wanted to be there for my family, so my schedule was their schedule. I left when they left, came home when they came home, and school bus drivers had taken over the carpooling! It was terrifying embarking on this new adventure, but I did it. I made law review and was in the top 12 percent of my class at Fordham Law School.

That was over twenty-five years ago now, and it was a decision that has brought tremendous reward and satisfaction. I never gave up my most important job of being a mom. Even though they're all grown up now and married with kids, they have always been, and remain, my first priority. But pursuing my own purpose has added to that a deep sense of personal satisfaction and reward. It was a choice that has been right for me.[7]

## PRINCIPLE #7: ENDURANCE

Finally, knowing and understanding your purpose will motivate you to endure. It will build in your life the tough, dogged determination never to quit, to face any and every challenge with a can-do spirit.

Endurance will build in you the character and the compassion not only to fulfill your purpose in life but to be the kind of person others look to as a role model, someone seasoned by life's challenges and able to win the race. Your purpose helps color the picture of what you are creating. This picture, coupled with keeping your focus on the journey rather than the destination, helps you endure.

Endurance training is something great athletes do so that their aerobic system can sustain prolonged physical activity. They follow a schedule of gradually increasing intensity. As soon as they are comfortable at one level of intensity, they ramp up the training, which forces the heart, lungs, and muscles to improve.

**Hope combines the determination to achieve your goals with the ability to generate the means to do so.**

Choosing to endure and continue in your purpose, like endurance training, creates the ability to produce power hour after hour. It becomes your fuel day after day, month after month, year after year, in spite of the setbacks and disappointments that will most certainly come.

These seven principles of purpose are in many ways the principles that I have chosen to live by. As my journey has taken on many twists and turns that have appeared at first glance to be so much different than what I thought, these principles have helped keep my hope alive.

Hope is one of life's greatest gifts. It is available to all of us, at all times, but we must choose to hold on to it no matter what we are facing. In his article "The Leadership Advantage," Warren Bennis tells us, "Exemplary leaders seem to expect success; they always anticipate positive outcomes. The glass for them is not simply full but brimming."

Hope combines the determination to achieve your goals with the ability to generate the means to do so. Hopeful people describe themselves with such statements as these:

- "I can think of ways to get out of a jam."
- "I energetically pursue my goals."
- "My experience has prepared me well for the future."
- "There are ways around any problem."[8]

## Different Than What I Thought, Better Than What I Imagined

No one can give hope to you. You have to find it and take it for yourself. I am striving to be a woman who has hope for things still unseen—in my career, my family, and my dreams.

There are things that fan hope into flame and make it stronger. There are also things that diminish or even kill it. The older I get, the more cautious I am about permitting things into my heart and mind that diminish hope, such as

- negative thoughts;
- focusing on what something looks like instead of what it can become;
- going through everyday motions instead of taking new risks; and
- people who are broken and therefore criticize my hope for what is yet in store.

Every day I must choose to believe. I also must realize that I see only a small portion of what my life is becoming at any given time. Though I have dreams and walk in my life purpose, there is no way to possibly grasp the breadth and depth of what I am becoming. Neither can you.

This is where my faith and spiritual beliefs kick in real benefits. I believe that God is in charge of everything and that His greater plans will ultimately prevail. In fact, one of the gifts this belief affords me is the realization that all of life's little twists and turns, trials and errors, are truly some of the best gifts. Though I would not choose them for myself, later on I am very grateful for each of them.

Fanny Crosby shared this belief. She was left blind at six weeks old as a result of careless medical treatment given by a man posing as a doctor. In spite of her blindness, she wrote more than nine thousand hymns in her ninety-five years and was a beloved poet. She always credited her blindness as a gift that helped the words flow from her pen.

Surprisingly, Fanny was never bitter about the stranger who left her blind. She wrote, "I have not for a moment in more than eighty-five years felt a spark of resentment against him, because I have always believed . . . that the good Lord by this means consecrated me to the work that I am still permitted to do."

In all my playtimes with Barbie and Ken as a young girl, I never envisioned being single until I was forty-two and then marrying a divorced man with four sons. When I finally met Ron, I was amazed at how so many prior experiences—some welcomed, others despised—had masterfully prepared me in surprising ways. All those years at the university with dozens of students, many of them guys, dropping by my office to talk about life had prepared me to be a stepmother to four sons. How else would I, as a single woman who never had a brother, know or understand even a little bit about young men? There was an unseen plan at work all along, preparing me for this surprise gift.

> **Sometimes our deepest longings bring us things we want and need but don't even know how to ask for.**

So, my friend, choose hope. Celebrate the many gifts in your life. Have you counted them lately? Are you familiar with the unique attributes of each one? Have you meditated on the wonder of how sometimes our deepest longings bring us things we want and need but don't even know how to ask for?

If it isn't already, your life is going to be surprisingly different than what you thought it would be. Still, your life is a gift, unlike anyone else's, waiting to be celebrated.

I leave you with a story that Bonnie St. John often shares.

> People ask me, "How does a one-legged African-American girl from San Diego become an Olympic ski racer winning silver and bronze at the 1984 Paralympics?" I tell them I've been able to overcome tremendous challenges because people along the way helped me push through limits:
>
> • the nurse who pushed me through painful hours of therapy after my leg was cut off at age five;
> • my ski coach who didn't give up on me when I broke my only leg and ran out of money; and
> • my boss in the White House who expected me to lead teams of economists who were older and smarter than me.
>
> Now it's my turn to make a difference in others' lives. I want to help them find the courage and spirit they need in order to live without limits.[9]

What a noble aspiration. I know you have one too. Like Bonnie and so many others, you and I must keep climbing toward our dreams no matter what life brings us. The climb will not always be easy, but success and satisfaction await, not only at the top, but also along every rung.

I close by simply saying *thank you*. Thank you for staying in the race and continuing the climb. For hoping when you feel hopeless. For investing in others and pushing them toward greatness. For being excellent and setting a standard of success that goes beyond money and job description. For being a woman others look to for a picture of how rich life can be.

You are a gift to the world. So put on whatever shoes make you feel beautiful. We are in this climb together, cheering one another on each step of the way.

# NOTES

## WOMEN AND OUR SHOES

1. NPD Group, "NPD Reports U.S. Footwear Industry Takes a Big Step Forward in 2005," February 10, 2006, http://www.npd.com/dynamic/releases/press_060210.html.

2. U.S. Department of Labor and Statistics, "101 Facts on the Status of Working Women," http://www.bpwusa.org/files/public/101FactsonWorkingWomen2005.pdf.pdf.

## CHAPTER 1: WHY AM I WORKING?

1. The Barna Group, "The Year's Most Intriguing Findings from Barna Research Studies," http://www.barna.org/FlexPage.aspx?Page=BarnaUpdate&BarnaUpdateID=77.

2. Os Guinness, *The Call: Finding and Fulfilling the Central Purpose of Your Life,* quoted in Idelette McVicker, "Finding Purpose," *Women Today,* http://www.womentodaymagazine.com/selfesteem/purpose.html.

3. Anne Page, interview with author, April 2006.

4. *Merriam-Webster Online,* s.v. "purpose," http://www.m-w.com/dictionary/purpose.

5. *Merriam-Webster Online,* s.v. "mission," http://www.m-w.com/dictionary/mission.

6. Bridgette Heller, interview with author, April 2006.

7. Accel-Team, "Employee Motivation in the Workplace," 2005, http://www.accel-team.com/human_relations/hrels_06_mcclelland.html.

8. Bonnie St. John, interview with author, April 2006.

## CHAPTER 2: THESE PEOPLE ARE DRIVING ME CRAZY!

1. *Merriam-Webster Online,* s.v. "whole," http://www.m-w.com/dictionary/whole.

2. This excerpt is reprinted by permission from CareerJournal.com ©2006 Dow Jones & Co. Inc. All rights reserved.

3. This excerpt is reprinted by permission from CareerJournal.com ©2006 Dow Jones & Co. Inc. All rights reserved.

4. Ibid.

5. Ibid.

6. Cecily Truett, interview with author, April 2006.

7. Mary Bellofatto, interview with author, April 2006.

8. Ibid.

## CHAPTER 3: NO ONE APPRECIATES ME AROUND HERE!

1. Towers Perrin and Gang & Gang, "Working Today: Exploring Employees' Emotional Connections to Their Jobs," 2003, http://www.towersperrin.com/hrservices/webcache /towers/United_States/publications/Reports/Working_Today_Exploring_Employees _Emotional_Connection_to_Their_Jobs/Work_experience.pdf.
2. Andrea Baumann Lustig, interview with author, April 2006.
3. Betty Lehan Harragan, *Games Mother Never Taught You*, rev. ed. (New York: Warner Books, 1989), 82.
4. Cathy Benko, interview with author, April 2006.
5. Richard Feynman, quoted in Tom Peters, *Leadership* (New York: DK Publishing, 2005), 141–42.
6. Westina Matthews Shatteen, interview with author, April 2006.
7. Todd Duncan, *Time Traps* (Nashville: Nelson, 2004), 89.
8. Barbara Walters, quoted in Patricia Fripp, "You Never Know Where Your Next Big Break Is Coming From!" Fripp.com, http://www.fripp.com/art.bigbreak.html.
9. Mary Bellofatto, interview with author, April 2006.

## CHAPTER 4: IS THIS ALL I'M WORKING FOR? THERE MUST BE SOMETHING MORE!

1. Louise Story, "Many Women at Elite Colleges Set Career Path to Motherhood," *New York Times*, September 20, 2005.
2. Consumer Credit Counseling Service, "Credit Counseling Statistics: You Are Not Alone!" 2005, http://www.creditcounselingbiz.com/credit_counseling_statistics.htm.
3. J. K. Rowling, interview with Katie Couric, MSNBC, December 8, 2003, http://www.msnbc.msn.com/id/3080035/.
4. *Online Dating Magazine*, "More Than 70% of Singles Ready to Commit," Online Dating Magazine.com, 1 April 2004, http://www.onlinedatingmagazine.com/news2004 /readytocommit.html.
5. National Center for Health Statistics, quoted in "Divorce Rates," Americans for Divorce Reform, http://www.divorcereform.org/rates.html.
6. Cheryl Cutlip, interview with author, April 2006.
7. Westina Matthews Shatteen, interview with author, April 2006.
8. Glenn Van Ekeren, *Speaker's Sourcebook II* (New York: Penguin, 1994), 207.
9. Wikipedia contributors, "Post-it Note," *Wikipedia, the Free Encyclopedia*, http://en.wikipedia.org/w/index.php?title=Post-it_note&oldid=51624722.
10. Denise Johnston, interview with author, April 2006.
11. Cheryl Cutlip, interview with author, April 2006.
12. *Fortune*'s "America's Top Most Admired Companies," 2006, http://money.cnn.com/magazines/fortune/mostadmired/best_worst/.

## CHAPTER 5: I'M UNRECOGNIZED, UNAPPRECIATED, AND UNDERPAID!

1. "Build a More Meaningful Career," Planet Job Info.com, http://www.planet-job.info/.
2. Joyce Roche, interview with author, April 2006.

# Notes

3. Corinne McLaughlin, "Women-Business-Spirituality: A New Formula for Leadership," http://www.womenbusinessspirituality.com/comments.html.

4. Lisa Sloan-Walker, interview with Karin Halperin, "Five Ways Women Can Raise Their Professional Profile," CareerJournal.com, 17 October 2005, http://www.careerjournal.com /myc/climbing/20051017-halperin.html?mod=RSS_Career_Journal&cjrss=frontpage. Accessed October 17, 2005.

5. Andrea Baumann Lustig, interview with author, April 2006.

6. Keith Regan, "AT&T Plans to Spend Millions to Re-launch Brand," *Tech News World,* December 30, 2005, http://www.technewsworld.com/story/rYZ8RP8qO2vJGB/ATT-Plans-to-Spend-Millions-to-Re-launch-Brand.xhtml.

7. Lisa Marks, interview with author, April 2006.

8. FAST COMPANY by TOM PETERS. Copyright 1997 by MANSUETO VENTURES LLC. Reproduced with permission of MANSUETO VENTURES LLC in the format Other Book via Copyright Clearance Center.

9. Ibid.

## CHAPTER 6: HOW DO I GET FROM "GREAT IDEA" TO "DREAM COME TRUE"?

1. John Carver, *Boards That Make a Difference: A New Design for Leadership in Nonprofit and Public Organizations* (New York: Jossey-Bass, 2006), 1.

2. Doug Eadie, *Extraordinary Board Leadership: The Seven Keys to High-Impact Governance* (Boston: Jones & Bartlett, 2000), 6–7.

3. Mark Joyner, *The Irresistible Offer: How to Sell Your Product or Service in 3 Seconds or Less* (Hoboken, NJ: John Wiley & Sons, 2005), 7.

4. Gabriela Ferrari, interview with author, May 2006.

5. Florence Littauer, *A Letter Is a Gift Forever: The Charm and Tradition of a Handwritten Note* (Eugene, OR: Harvest House, 2001), 55.

6. Alexandra Stoddard, *Gift of a Letter* (New York: HarperCollins, 1991).

7. Littauer, *A Letter Is a Gift Forever,* 61.

## CHAPTER 7: CAN I REALLY THRIVE IN LEADERSHIP?

1. Max Depree, *Leadership Is an Art* (New York: Dell, a division of Random House, 1990), 13.

2. Peter Drucker, *The Effective Executive: The Definitive Guide for Getting the Right Things Done* (New York: HarperCollins, 2002).

3. Laurie Beth Jones, *The Path: Creating Your Mission Statement for Work and for Life* (New York: Hyperion, 1998).

4. Sylvia Hatchell, interview with author, April 2006.

5. John C. Maxwell, *The 360 Degree Leader: Developing Your Influence from Anywhere in the Organization* (Nashville: Nelson Business, 2006), 268.

6. Drucker, *Effective Executive,* 29.

7. Gabriela Ferrari, interview with author May 2006.

8. Drucker, quoted in "Quotes about Limitations," Zaadz, http://www.zaadz.com/quotes /topics/limitations?size=grande.

## CHAPTER 8: WHO, ME? SPEAK IN PUBLIC?

1. Carla Kimball, interview with author, April 2006.
2. Patricia Fripp, "Add Credibility to Your Business Reputation Through Public Speaking," Fripp.com, http://fripp.com/art.addcred.html.
3. *The Book of Lists*, quoted in "Overcoming the FEAR of Public Speaking," LeadershipSpeaking.com, http://www.leadershipspeaking.com/speaker_fear.htm.
4. Sonya Hamlin, *How to Talk So People Will Listen* (New York: HarperCollins, 2006), 47.
5. Chevy Nova Awards, quoted in Rick Luquette, http://humor.luquette.org/chevy_nova_awards.htm.
6. Hamlin, *How to Talk*, 19–20.
7. Ibid., 211–12.
8. Celina Realuyo, interview with author, April 2006.
9. Bonnie St. John, interview with author, April 2006.
10. U.S. Department of Health, Education, and Welfare, quoted by Glenn Van Ekeren, *Speaker's Sourcebook II* (New York: Penguin, 1994), 119.
11. Carla Kimball, interview with author, April 2006.
12. Zig Ziglar, *Zig Ziglar's Little Book of Big Quotes* (Dallas, TX: Zig Ziglar Corporation, 2004).

## CHAPTER 9: I NEED GREAT MENTORS, BUT ISN'T EVERYONE JUST TOO BUSY?

1. Tom Peters, *Leadership* (NY: DK Publishing, 2005), 145.
2. Carole Hyatt, interview with author, April 2006.
3. Donald Trump, interview with Larry King on *Larry King Live*, March 9, 2006, http://transcripts.cnn.com/TRANSCRIPTS/0603/09/lkl.01.html.
4. Carole Hyatt, interview with author, April 2006.
5. LEARNING FROM OTHER WOMEN by DUFF, CAROLYN S. Copyright 2006 by AMACOM BOOKS. Reproduced with permission of AMACOM BOOKS in the format Other Book via Copyright Clearance Center.
6. Charlie "Tremendous" Jones, "Books Are My Favorite Mentors," ExecutiveBooks.com, http://www.executivebooks.com/cjones/cj_BookMentors.html. Used by permission.
7. Denise Johnston, interview with author, April 2006.
8. Cathy Benko, interview with author, April 2006.
9. Joyce Roche, interview with author, April 2006.

## CHAPTER 10: DIFFERENT THAN WHAT I THOUGHT, BETTER THAN WHAT I IMAGINED

1. Diana Ingram, interview with author, April 2006.
2. Martha Stewart, *Martha Rules* (New York: Rodale, 2005), 157. Reprinted from: Martha Rules © 2005 by Martha Stewart. Permission granted by Rodale, Inc., Emmaus, PA 18098. Available wherever books are sold or directly from the publisher by calling (800) 848-4735.
3. Kathi, e-mail to author, April 2006.
4. Mother Teresa quoted in Carol Kelly-Gangi, ed., *Mother Teresa: Her Essential Wisdom* (New York: Barnes & Noble, 2006), 6.

# Notes

5. Viktor Frankl, *Man's Search for Meaning* (Boston: Beacon, 1992), quoted in International Network of Personal Meaning.com, http://www.meaning.ca/meaning_therapy /viktor_frankl.html.

6. Jillian Donnelly, "Respect Is the Key to Job Satisfaction for Women," CareerJournal.com, 2003, http://www.careerwomen.com/pr_satisfaction052803.jsp.

7. Debora Grobman, interview with author, April 2006.

8. Warren Bennis, "The Leadership Advantage," *Leader to Leader Institute.* 12 (Spring 1999): 18–23.

9. Bonnie St. John, interview with author, April 2006.

# ABOUT THE AUTHOR

Lynette Lewis has been inspiring women on the topics of vision and purpose for over twenty years. Her eclectic career has taken her from PR and fundraising at a major university to the senior marketing leader for the National Women's Initiative at Deloitte in New York City. Lynette maintains an active speaking schedule through Maxwell's Maximum Impact Speakers bureau and many national and international corporate women's forums.

For information on other Lynette Lewis resources,
or to schedule Lynette as a speaker,
workshop leader, or consultant, please visit
www.lynettelewis.com.